Diane Clark's
MICROWAVE COOKBOOK

Diane Clark's

MICROWAVE COOKBOOK

HAWTHORN/DUTTON
NEW YORK

Photographs by Tom Landen

For information contact: Elsevier-Dutton Publishing Co., Inc., 2 Park Avenue, New York, N.Y. 10016

Library of Congress Cataloging in Publication Data
Clark, Diane.
   Diane Clark's Microwave cookbook.

   1. Microwave cookery.   I. Title.   II. Title:
Microwave cookbook.
TX832.C56   641.5′882   80-22958

ISBN: 0-8015-2023-1

Published simultaneously in Canada by Clarke, Irwin & Company Limited, Toronto and Vancouver

10 9 8 7 6 5 4 3 2 1

First Edition

Preface

Writing this book has been a joy—and a chore. The joy has been the people I have had the pleasure of working with. The chore was in executing recipes over and over and over until they were just right. But even that was rewarding when the ingredients, power setting, and cooking time came together in one perfect dish.

I have dedicated the past four years to learning everything possible about microwave cooking. Originally, the intent was to share this information with my cooking classes. But the idea grew into cooking features for WBTV (Charlotte, North Carolina) and a weekly column, "Microwave Methods," in *The Charlotte News*.

From all these different areas, one question has been asked repeatedly: "What cookbooks can you recommend?" Since microwave cooking has only recently become a viable method of primary cooking, there are not as many books available to us as there are for conventional ovens. Writing this book seemed to be the best way to share what I have learned from many different sources. Besides, there is so much to tell that this is the only way to do it all at once.

My special thanks and appreciation go to Jonellen Heckler. She is always there to say, "Yes, you can." As a writer, Jonellen has followed encouragement with practical advice on what to do with what you've done. Thank you, Jonellen.

And then there are my neighbors and friends who have always been brave enough to sample the latest experiment. Their courage and comments were very helpful.

I am most grateful to my family—Mason, Jennifer, and Elizabeth. They have had to eat all kinds of things that, left to their own devices, would never have been put on the table.

v

They've put up with a messy kitchen, dusty house, and late car pools because Mom was typing. And they never once complained. In fact, they have cleaned the kitchen, dusted the house, and helped in any way they could so that this book would be a reality.

The cliché may be old but it is appropriate—this has been a labor of love. May it bring you many pleasurable meals and more free time out of the kitchen to enjoy every day.

DIANE P. CLARK

Contents

WHAT'S COOKING?

HERE'S HOW AND WHY

1. General Introduction

Conventional ovens cook by surrounding food with hot, dry air. Microwave ovens cook by heat produced within the food itself. Here's how it happens and why you need to know.

Electrical current flows into the oven and passes through a tube called a magnetron. The magnetron converts electrical energy into microwaves, which are fed into the oven cavity. Microwaves can travel only in a straight line so there is a fan (stirrer) to blow them around and bounce them off all the oven surfaces. If the pattern is not even, cooking will not be even and it will be necessary to rotate dishes during the cooking period.

Three things can happen to a microwave after it is in the oven. It can be absorbed, transmitted, or reflected.

ABSORBED: Microwaves are attracted to fat, sugar, and water molecules in food. They penetrate approximately ¾ inch of the outer edge of the food and cause the molecules to vibrate. As they vibrate, heat is produced. The heat is conducted to the center very much like a string of dominoes knocking into each other. Remember—all cooking begins at the outer edge and the center is the last portion to cook. That is why stirring with a spoon, whenever possible, is required for even cooking.

TRANSMITTED: Microwaves pass straight through items with no fat, sugar, or moisture and have absolutely no effect on them. That is why you can cook with many different materials. The oven does not heat the dish. The dish may be warm because it has pulled heat from the food.

REFLECTED: Microwaves cannot pass through metal; they bounce off it. If food were completely enclosed in metal or foil, no cooking would occur. However, the finish on the oven walls would be damaged and the lifespan of the magnetron shortened.

Conventional cooking is figured in terms of temperature. Microwave cooking is always by time—never temperature. A probe or microwave thermometer senses the temperature of the food, not the oven. If you understand what affects the time required for food to cook, it will be easier to know how to cook. Factors affecting time include:

STARTING TEMPERATURE: Is the food straight from the refrigerator and cold or has it come to room temperature? The warmer it is to start with, the faster it will cook.
VOLUME: Each piece of food cooks itself. One potato may cook in 4 minutes but two potatoes will take 8 minutes.
DENSITY: How dense is the food? A loaf of bread will heat more quickly than a roast of equal size.
FAT, SUGAR, MOISTURE: Foods high in fat or sugar cook rapidly. Foods high in moisture content cook more slowly.
ARRANGEMENT: The outer edge of a dish receives the longest cooking time. Arrange the portion of the food requiring the longest cooking time on the outer edge.
STIRRING: Stirring food moves what is on the outer edge to the center and vice versa. This equalizes the amount of cooking received by all parts of the food. If stirring is neglected, the outer portion may overcook and the center undercook.

The amount of time required to cook any given recipe may vary. That is why recipes often give a general time. Just as your conventional oven may be slow or fast, the same can hold true for a microwave. How much electrical power is coming into the house affects the oven. If you are fixing dinner at the same time as most other people in your neighborhood, less electricity is coming into the oven and it will cook a little more slowly.

When a recipe says to "tightly cover" a dish it is important to do so. The covering prevents food from drying out and spreads the heat evenly. Plastic wrap does the best job and need not be punctured. Allowing steam to escape defeats the purpose for using it.

Glass lids are satisfactory for reheating but do not form a tight seal. Waxed paper and paper towels accomplish little other than reducing splatters.

The containers for cooking have a separate section devoted solely to their description. You probably own most of what is necessary. The only special accessory that is an absolute "must" is a roasting rack. It is usually made of hard plastic, has ridges,

The way food is arranged in the dish affects how well it cooks. Note how the small tips of the pork chops are placed in the center portion of the dish.

A roasting rack is the only special accessory that is absolutely necessary. It will allow the grease to drain from bacon and will prevent stewing a roast in its own juices.

and can be set inside a baking dish. The purpose is to keep meat out of its juices as it cooks. Its importance is further explained in the section on meat.

An accessory that is expensive and unnecessary is the browning dish. Use a skillet or frying pan to accomplish the same thing.

If your oven is not equipped with a temperature probe, you may want to invest in a microwave thermometer. Regular thermometers cannot be used because the microwaves are reflected off the mercury. A candy thermometer for microwaves may soon be available, if it is not by the time this book goes to press. It will open up a whole new experience in candy making for microwave cooks, so plan to start a regular exercise program the day you buy one.

Dish size is often specified in the recipe. If it is not, choose a dish that will be one-half to two-thirds full with the ingredients. Filled to the brim, it may boil over. A mixture that is spread too thin may overcook.

Two elements are essential for good results and can never be overemphasized. Number one: be conservative in cooking time. Always use the least amount of time called for in a recipe. If it is undercooked, you can put it back in and continue cooking. An overcooked dish can only be chalked up to experience and down to indigestion. Number two: allow for standing time, which is actually carry-over cooking. Food is not done when it comes out of the microwave. The molecules continue to vibrate and produce heat. The more dense the food, the longer the standing time. Food that is completely cooked when it is removed from the oven stands a good chance of being overcooked by the time it is eaten.

A microwave oven that is used is an oven that will get dirty. Food splatters and some dishes boil over for even the most careful cook. The big surprise is how easily it cleans. There is no heat to bake the food onto the surfaces. They wipe clean with a damp sponge. More stubborn spots can be softened by the moisture created from a cup of boiling water. Never use an abrasive pad or powder that would scratch the soft finish on oven walls.

2. Power Settings

You would never cook all your food under the broiler of a conventional oven, and you should never cook all your food on High in a microwave oven. In this collection of recipes you will find different percentages of power, which are the equivalent of different temperatures in a conventional oven. However, microwave manufacturers are not as standard in their labeling as would be desirable. If you are not already thinking in terms of % of power, refer to the accompanying chart. It will clarify the recipes in this book and those from other sources.

Percentage of power	Frequently used name	Time required for 1 cup of lukewarm water to boil
100%	High	2–2½ minutes
70%	Medium High	3½–4½ minutes
	Roast	
50%	Medium	4½–5½ minutes
	Simmer	
30%	Medium Low	8½–10 minutes
	Low	
	Defrost	
10%	Low	more than 10 minutes
	Warm	

3. Dishes

Part of the fun of microwave cooking is all the different types of containers that can be used. Clean-up is easier if not nonexistent. The following list is a guideline for what can or cannot be used in a microwave.

OVEN-PROOF GLASSWARE: Commonly referred to by the brand name Pyrex, it is available in a wide variety of shapes and sizes and is inexpensive when compared to pots and pans. Round bowls, measuring cups, casseroles, platters, custard cups, and ring molds are basic cooking containers.

GLASS-CERAMIC: Commonly referred to by the brand name Corning. Do not use any pieces with metal. Starchy foods tend to stick.

PLASTIC: Many containers are being manufactured in a hard plastic specifically for microwave ovens. Any plastics marked dishwasher-safe are microwave-safe. Bowls such as margarine or whipped toppings are packaged in are suitable for storing and reheating leftovers, but prolonged cooking or use with high-acid foods is not recommended. Do not use Melamine dishes. Heat-sealed plastic bags are usable if they are punctured to allow for expansion.

PAPER: Paper plates can be used. Plastic-coated paper containers

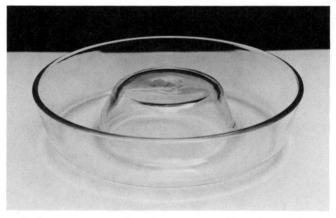

Oven-proof glassware is perfect for microwave cooking. The ring mold eliminates undercooked centers in foods ranging from quick breads to meatloaves.

have been developed for microwave cooking and can also be used in conventional ovens. Frozen food packed in cardboard can be cooked in the box if it is not lined with foil. Recycled paper contains metal and should not be used. Newspaper should not be used as the printer's ink may cause a fire.

METAL: Pots and pans are definitely not used. Dishes trimmed with gold, silver, or platinum fall into this category as well. Check the bottom of a dish or bowl to be sure there is no gold signature. Lead crystal does have lead in it and cannot be used.

ALUMINUM FOIL: TV dinner trays no more than ¾-inch deep can be used if the top layer of foil is removed. Deeper dishes, such as those used for pot pies, are unsatisfactory. Compartmented trays are available in plastic and plastic foam and are more practical. Small amounts of foil are used for shielding during defrosting or cooking. The amount of foil used should never exceed half the surface area of the food. Keep all metal at least 1 inch away from the sides of the oven.

CLAY COOKERS: Can be used. Follow manufacturer's instructions for presoaking container in water.

POTTERY, STONEWARE, CHINA: Most new dishes state whether or not they can be used in a microwave. If uncertain, use the dish test given at the end of this section.

WOOD AND STRAW: Not recommended. In due time, the moisture will be removed and the wood or straw will crack. Wooden spoons can be left in a bowl for stirring but may become hot.

SEASHELLS: Perfect for seafood dishes.

FOOD SHELLS: Pineapple, orange, grapefruit, melon, pepper, squash. Use your imagination for a container that is both attractive and disposable.

If you have doubt as to whether or not a dish or bowl may be safely used, there is a test. First, be sure there is no metal on the container. Place it in the microwave oven and set a small cup of water in a corner. Run the oven on High for 30 seconds. If the dish feels warm at the end of this time, don't use it. There is a metallic content in the glaze or clay. Conduct the test before the oven has been used for cooking; otherwise, the bottom of the oven may be warm and will transfer heat to the dish.

4. Defrosting

The microwave oven will thaw frozen food and not begin the cooking process if accurate times and settings are used. Here are a few tips for the best results:

1. Do not defrost food on a plastic foam tray. It acts as an insulator.
2. If food items are stacked (chops, bacon, etc.), separate them as soon as possible.
3. Turn food over halfway through for even thawing.
4. Freezing ground beef in the shape of a doughnut will allow it to defrost without cooking the edges.
5. To check a roast, insert a sharp knife to the center.
6. Allow a standing time to complete thawing. This avoids cooking the outer edges.
7. Food must be completely defrosted for even cooking. Otherwise, thawed portions will overcook and icy portions will undercook.

Ground beef frozen in the shape of a dough-nut will defrost evenly.

5. Appetizers and Snacks

The most successful entertaining is done by hosts and hostesses who enjoy their own parties. A nervous, overworked hostess may make her guests feel guilty; as if it were their fault she had to work so hard! With careful planning, you can be a guest at your own party and create a relaxed atmosphere for everyone.

Those delicious little appetizers often mean long stays in the kitchen or unappealingly cold "hot" hors d'oeuvres. Let the microwave change all that. First, experiment with one or two to be certain of time, power setting, and if in fact they do well in the microwave. Many hors d'oeuvres can be prepared in advance and reheated on an oven-proof serving platter. Crackers with a topping should not be assembled in advance as they tend to become soggy. Toothpicks and wooden skewers go into the oven right along with the food. Watch the time carefully. Only seconds may be required for heating—not minutes.

The power setting used will depend on the ingredients. Water chestnuts wrapped in bacon and splashed with Worcestershire sauce will cook on High. Stuffed mushrooms, sour cream dips, or shellfish require a more gentle 70% power.

Cheese is most flavorful when served at room temperature. The time from refrigerator to serving can be greatly reduced by using a 10% power setting in the microwave. Unexpected company need not create a problem in the food department. Top a cracker with a thin piece of cheese and an olive slice and pop a plate full in the oven at 70% power. Another quick and tasty cheese snack can be made with a bar of processed American cheese. Cut a 1-pound bar into cubes and melt at 70% power. Stir in one-half to one full can of Mexican jalapeño relish and serve with sturdy chips and plenty of cold drinks. When the dip cools, return bowl to oven and reheat.

Nuts are easier to shell with the aid of a microwave. Place 2 cups of nuts in 1 cup of water. Cook on High for 5 minutes and then shell.

Poor results are obtained with popcorn even if a special popper is used. If you have a regular popcorn popper, use it. Should there be any leftovers, they can be freshened up in the oven the next day.

6. Beverages

Bringing water to a boil takes as long in the microwave as it does on the stove. Reasons for doing it in the microwave are convenience, safety, and keeping the kitchen cool in the summer.

If you're rushing out to the car in the morning, heat the water for coffee in a Styrofoam cup. Adding the instant coffee after the water has boiled will avoid a bitter taste. If you make a pot of coffee, store the leftover in the refrigerator or freeze in ice cube trays. When it is reheated in the microwave it will taste fresh from the pot.

When making hot chocolate try adding a marshmallow during the last 25 seconds. Young children can fix their own as there is no danger of touching a hot burner. If you use milk rather than water, fill the cup only two-thirds full to avoid a boil-over and heat at 70% power.

Starting temperature will affect how quickly a beverage heats. Hot tap water will boil sooner than cold.

Large quantities of liquid can be heated in an oven-proof pitcher, but never heat a liquid in a narrow-neck bottle. If you are uncertain as to how long a beverage needs to be heated, use the temperature probe set to 140° to 160°.

A professional baker shared her secret for cutting the price of tea in half, and it does work! For 1 gallon of iced tea, combine 2 cups of water, 4 tea bags, and ½ teaspoon of baking soda. Cook on High for 4 minutes. After the tea has steeped, squeeze the bags to release all the flavor before they are discarded. Stir in sugar and lemon juice to taste and 3½ quarts of cold water. The baking soda releases more flavor from the tea without leaving any flavor of its own. When brewing tea, do not allow the water to boil because that produces a slightly bitter taste.

Milk boils vigorously in a microwave oven. One cup of milk in a measure of equal size will boil over. It is best to place the one cup of milk in a larger, four-cup measure.

7. Soup

We are so accustomed to opening a can for soup that homemade could almost qualify for an endangered species list. Soup is easy to make and the flavor far superior to anything you might have imagined.

Here are a few pointers to keep in mind. Always use a container large enough to prevent boiling over. An oven-safe tureen would be convenient for cooking and attractive for serving. Soup can be reheated in individual bowls or crocks. A cover is not necessary during cooking as there is little moisture lost. Many soups are started on High and simmered at 60% to 50% power to allow flavors to blend. If the soup contains milk or wine, do not allow it to boil. Wine brings out the saltiness in foods so add less salt than seems necessary. Meat and vegetables should be chopped in small pieces for quick, even cooking. Dried beans will not cook well and canned beans should be substituted.

Whether the soup is from a can or homemade, one plastic bowl can be used for storing, reheating, and eating. A great way to save on clean-up time.

8. Yeast Breads

Baking bread for your family is a wonderful way to say, "I love you." But with the hectic schedule most homemakers and career women follow, it is almost impossible to find time to do it. I would never suggest baking bread in the microwave because there is no browning or crusting. I will encourage you to proof the dough in the microwave. The rising of the dough is usually measured in hours but it can be done in less than one hour in the microwave.

Yeast is proofed in water that must be warm—about 110°—and can be tested like a baby's bottle. Yeast will not react properly if the water is either too hot or too cold. Do add at least a pinch of sugar to the water for the yeast to feed on since it is a growing organism.

You should be just as careful about the temperature of any milk or water added to the dough as the preparation progresses.

Proofing bread dough in the microwave can be a great time-saver. Place the dough in an oven-proof bowl large enough to allow it to double in size.

The yeast must be kept alive and healthy. Use the microwave to take the chill off the milk but be careful not to overdo it: 30 seconds will probably be about right for 1 cup of milk.

Combine the ingredients according to recipe instructions. Kneading may be done with a mixer and dough hook, food processor, or by hand. The hand method requires pushing with the base of the palms, and don't worry about kneading the dough too much—it's virtually impossible. The dough will be shiny and have tiny bubbles under the surface when the job is done.

The next step is to grease a glass bowl large enough for the dough to double in volume. Grease the dough or turn it over in the bowl so that it is well coated. Cover the bowl with waxed paper and set it in a dish of hot water. Place it in the oven and program in 4 minutes at 10% power. Let it rest for 15 minutes. You will probably have to do this twice for the dough to double in size. As a test, make an indentation in the dough with your finger. If it stays, the dough is right.

Now it is time to punch the dough down, and that is exactly what you do. Place the dough on a board and give it a good punch with your fist right in the center.

Shape the dough into a greased glass loaf pan. Tent it with waxed paper, set it in a baking dish of hot water, and repeat the rising process until the loaf has doubled in size. Dough that does not rise enough will be heavy after baking. Dough that has risen

Make an indentation in the dough with your finger. If it stays, the dough is ready for the next step.

too much will collapse during baking. Watch it carefully to find the happy medium.

Make your decision as to whether the bread will be baked conventionally or microwaved. If you choose the conventional method, a glass loaf pan will require a lower heat. Reduce it about 25 degrees. If you use the microwave, remove the dish of water before baking.

Microwaved bread should be stored in an airtight container. Without a crust it will dry out very quickly.

Punch the dough down and place it in an oven-proof loaf pan to rise again.

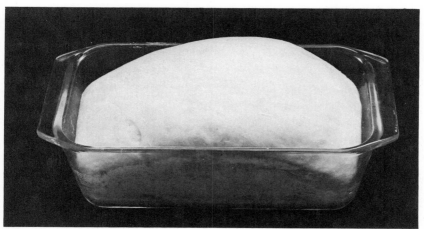

After the second rising, the bread may be baked in a microwave or conventional oven. If baked conventionally, lower the temperature by 25° to allow for the glass, rather than metal, loaf pan.

9. Reheating Bread

When reheating bread of any type, it must be wrapped in a towel. Paper towels or linen tea towels work very well. If the bread has a sticky topping and cannot be wrapped, at least set it on top of a paper towel. The towel, not the bread, will absorb the moisture in the oven.

Touching the top of a roll or a biscuit will not reveal its warmth. The crust is dry and will remain cool. The interior is moist and warms quickly. It only takes seconds, not minutes.

10. Fish

Fish defrosts quickly and easily using the microwave oven but it is a two-step process. First, thaw the fish partially in the oven. Finish by running cold water over it. Relying on the oven for total thawing would toughen the edges.

While meats are prepared first and allowed to stand, fish is not. Seafoods cool very quickly and do not reheat well. They are cooked last.

If juices coagulate when baking a fillet, try lining the dish with a paper towel. If you are baking "the catch of the day" whole, protect the head and tail with aluminum foil.

The connective tissue of fish is very fragile and can easily overcook. Plastic wrap tightly sealed over the dish retains steam and keeps fish very moist.

Most fish is cooked quickly on High. The exceptions are clams, scallops, and oysters. These are done on 70% power. Shellfish require the same amount of time to cook with or without the shell.

To test for doneness, lift the fish gently from the center with a fork. There should be a slight resistance to flaking. The outer edge will be opaque and the center translucent.

Seafood may leave an odor in the oven. To freshen the oven and the kitchen, boil 1 cup of water with ¼ cup of lemon juice and several whole cloves for 4 to 5 minutes.

11. Meat

Preparing meat in the microwave oven is a definite advantage when you have a limited amount of time for cooking. Done properly, this is also the best way to prepare the main portion of a meal. In a microwave oven there is no dry, hot air which can dry out meat. Meat will be juicier and have less shrinkage than when done conventionally.

Meat cooked for at least 10 minutes will brown. The degree of browning will vary according to the cut and fat content. If the color is not pleasing—and appearance is the first "taste"—do not despair. A more traditional coloring can be achieved by basting once before cooking with Kitchen Bouquet sauce, dry gravy or soup mix, soy sauce, Worcestershire sauce, steak sauce, or barbecue sauce. Simply choose the basting agent according to the flavor that blends best with the meal.

When it comes to seasonings, there are two rules. Number one: ELIMINATE THE USE OF SALT. Salt pulls the juices out of meat. It can be added, to taste, when served. Number two: go easy on spices, especially if they are hot. Flavors develop more fully in a microwave oven. As with the salt, more can be added later if necessary.

One special piece of equipment is necessary for cooking meats and that is a roasting rack. They are usually made of a hard plastic, have ridges so juices can drain, and fit inside a glass baking dish. A roast should be kept out of the juices while it cooks. If it is not, it will be either stewed on the bottom or overcooked in the high fat content of the liquid. Liquids which accumulate in the dish during cooking should be periodically removed with a basting tube so that the microwave energy is used to heat only the meat. Reserve what is needed to make gravy in a separate bowl. The rack is also handy for bacon and cut-up portions of meat which do not cook in a sauce.

Whole portions of meat, such as a roast or a ham, are cooked uncovered. (Any spatters on the oven are easily wiped off with a damp sponge.) Cut-up portions of meat, such as chops, chicken parts, or ribs, are tightly covered with plastic wrap. These pieces are thin and could dry out during the rapid cooking if moisture is not held in by the covering. The way cut-up portions are arranged in the dish is another factor in successful cooking. The thickest part must be on the outer edge of the dish and the thin part toward the center.

Standing time is essential for meat. It is still cooking after being removed from the oven. Cook the vegetables and warm the bread while it finishes. This way all the dishes can be hot and ready to serve at the same time.

Any meat can be prepared in the microwave oven. But there is one cut that is best done otherwise—steak. A charcoal grill is still best for steaks. If there are extra steaks in the freezer, sear them on the grill just short of being done, rewrap, and freeze. Then when you're in a hurry or there is snow on the ground and no one wants to be an outside chef, finish the steak in the microwave oven. The same can be done with hamburgers and hot dogs in order to enjoy grilled flavor with microwave convenience.

The same idea can be applied in reverse. To reduce the amount of time to cook ribs or poultry on the grill, begin cooking them in the microwave oven. When they are ready for barbecue sauce—the last 15 minutes—take them out to the grill. Again, the delicious flavor and convenience have been combined.

12. Ground Beef

Hamburger may well be the backbone of the American diet. Three grades of ground beef are generally available in the market. Each will do very well in a microwave as the grinding process has tenderized the meat. If you do have a choice, the middle grade will give the best results as it is neither too fat nor too lean.

To defrost ground beef without cooking the edges it must have been shaped correctly for freezing. A lump or pyramid shape is incorrect. When the meat is shaped like a doughnut, thawing will be even and quick since there is no mass in the center requiring additional time.

For recipes using browned beef there is a trick that makes the messy chore of draining grease obsolete. Crumble the beef into a plastic colander set in a glass pie plate. As it cooks, the grease drains into the dish and away from the meat. One pound will take about 6 minutes on High, uncovered. Stir twice during cooking so that it will be evenly done and broken up into small bits. If fine-ground beef is desired for a sauce or chili, run it through a food processor or blender. The color is lighter than that of beef browned in a frying pan but when mixed with other ingredients this will not be noticed.

The meatloaf may have been invented by the homemaker whose budget simply could not stretch far enough to buy a roast. After all, it does slice like a roast, late-night kitchen prowlers can use leftovers for a sandwich, and it is economical. The tradition can be carried on with the microwave by making a slight adjustment. Because corners overcook and dense foods tend to undercook in the center, a meatloaf is best prepared in a ring mold, bundt pan, or custard cups. A ring mold or bundt pan cooks evenly and creates an attractive dish. The meat can be unmolded and the center filled with potatoes or other vegetables. Individual servings in custard cups are handy for late arrivals at dinner or for freezing. A mini-loaf of ¼ pound will cook in approximately 1½ minutes on High. Color will come from the sauce or by adding a browning agent, such as Kitchen Bouquet sauce, to the meat mixture.

One pound of ground beef can be browned in approximately six minutes. Place the meat in a plastic colander set in an oven-proof pie plate. Note that the meat is spread away from the center to promote even cooking.

When the ground beef is browned, the grease will have drained into the dish. This helps eliminate a few extra calories.

Hamburger patties can also be done in the microwave oven. If six patties have been made from 1 pound of beef, one patty at room temperature will cook in 1 minute on High; one frozen patty will cook in 2 minutes on High. The color will be gray and rather unappealing. A browning dish can be used for a better color. It is just as easy to precook a large quantity of hamburgers in a frying pan or on a grill, freeze or store in the refrigerator, and reheat in the microwave.

Any ground beef that has been extended with crumbs or cereal will cook faster. Be sure to keep that in mind when converting recipes.

13. Roasts

The microwave oven can bring out the very best in any cut of meat if proper cooking methods are used. A tender cut of meat, such as a sirloin tip, will cook very quickly and without special preparation. A tougher cut, such as a chuck, will cook slowly in a liquid. Tomato- or wine-based marinades give a head start on breaking down tough tissues.

Weight should be taken into consideration. Is it large enough to cook at least 10 minutes so browning will occur? If more than 8 pounds, the result may be an overdone outer portion and an underdone center. Know the exact weight so the amount of cooking time can be figured correctly.

The shape of a roast affects how well it cooks. A thin section will cook more rapidly than thick portions, and shielding with aluminum foil may be necessary.

Bones can cause uneven cooking. If a bone cannot be removed, select a cut where it is well surrounded by meat to minimize the effect. A standing rib roast is best done in a conventional oven.

Well-marbled meat is tender and browns best. If there is a shortage of fat in or on the meat, consider laying on slices of bacon.

For even cooking, a roast should be round rather than oblong.

Defrosting meat in the microwave oven is terrific if you forgot to take it out of the freezer or have unexpected guests for dinner. Yet, it is a good practice in its own right. Meat thawed in the oven retains more of the juices. This increases tenderness and reduces shrinkage. Standing time applies to defrosting as well as to cooking. If there are ice crystals in the center portion, do not return it to the oven. The edges may begin to cook during prolonged defrosting. Better to let it stand at room temperature for a short time. To test for readiness, insert a sharp knife to the center of the meat. Meat must be completely thawed and preferably at room temperature. If not, you will end up over-cooking the warm area or undercooking the cold.

To cook a roast, season according to taste (minus salt), place on a roasting rack in a baking dish, and do not cover. Figure correct time and settings appropriate for the cut of meat from the book that came with the oven. The most accurate method for perfect doneness is to use a temperature probe. It is inserted during the second half of the cooking time. This eliminates all guesswork or mathematical errors. If the oven is not equipped with a probe, a thermometer specifically designed for microwave ovens can be used. Be certain the tip of the probe does not touch a bone or fat pocket which would produce an inaccurate reading. Temperatures should reach 125° for rare, 140° for medium, and 165° for well done. The internal temperature will rise another 10 to 15 degrees during standing time. If aluminum foil is used to hold in heat during standing time, it should be tented. Completely closed foil would hold in the steam and make the top wet.

Leftover roast need not be wasted if you just remember that it is in the refrigerator! Rather than place an entire piece of meat in the oven several times, slice off only what is wanted for a particular meal. Make the slices uniform in thickness, arrange in a circle on the plate and in one layer. If the meat has dried out, cover with gravy or a sauce. Use a minimal amount of time. One pound will reach serving temperature in approximately 1½ minutes.

An extra benefit to preparing a roast in the microwave oven: if some like it rare and others prefer medium to well done, that's how they shall have it. Cook the roast rare and slice off several pieces to cook a few more seconds. This is one time when you can indeed please everyone.

14. Stews

A bowl of hot stew is tasty, filling, nutritional, and economical. Those are a lot of good reasons to learn how to make a good stew. The more tender the meat to begin with, the better; but with proper handling even less tender meat can be delicious.

The first step in the preparation of a stew is to cut all the chunks of meat into a uniform size since each piece cooks individually. Small cubes will cook through more quickly than large cubes. During cooking, the bowl should be covered tightly with plastic wrap to hold in moisture and increase tenderness. Stirring at regular intervals is important for even cooking. The first 5 minutes of cooking should be done on High and then the power setting reduced to 50% or 30% for the remaining time. Fresh or frozen vegetables, also chopped uniformly, are added at the beginning, but canned or precooked vegetables are added later. For stews that are to be frozen, use flour or arrowroot to thicken the sauce as cornstarch tends to separate when frozen.

15. Pork, Ham, and Lamb

Any cuts of pork, ham, or lamb are cooked at 70% power to insure tenderness. Breakfast pork, such as bacon and sausage, is the exception and cooks on High.

The shape of whole cuts are often irregular, with one end thick and the other thin. The thin portion may be shielded with aluminum foil during the first half of cooking. Do not cover more than half the meat.

Pork loin or shoulder roasts should be tied with string to prevent the muscles from separating during cooking. The internal temperature of pork should reach 155° in the oven and will continue to rise to 170° during the standing time.

How many minutes per pound to cook a cured ham will vary. Different amounts of sugar are used for curing in each area of the country. Check a ham often to be sure it does not overcook. For a precooked ham, internal temperature should reach 120°.

Leg of lamb cooks better and carves more easily if the bone is removed and it is rolled like a roast. A butcher can do this for you.

Ribs and chops are done on a rack unless baked in a sauce. Arrange the pieces with the thickest portion on the outer edge of the dish and the thin portion toward the center. Cover the dish tightly with plastic wrap to prevent the meat from drying out during the cooking. Remember that ribs can be partially cooked in the microwave oven and finished on a charcoal grill. Allow one pound of ribs per person.

16. Poultry

Chicken can be served simply or extravagantly and lots of ways in between. It generally cooks in 6 to 8 minutes per pound on High. It should be so tender and moist that it almost melts in your mouth. Begin experimenting with Rock Cornish game hens, step up to chickens, and graduate to a turkey. The basic principles are the same for all—size is the only difference.

Let's begin here with a whole chicken. Fryers are the best choice as stewing hens have a thick, fatty skin. If the chicken is defrosted in the microwave, some shielding with foil may be necessary on the wings, ends of the drumsticks and the breastbone. These areas are thin and could begin to cook while the plumper portions are still thawing. The giblets should be removed as soon as they are loose and the juices drained. Ice crystals will remain in the cavity. Complete the thawing process by rinsing with cold water. Remember that a chicken unevenly thawed will be a chicken unevenly cooked.

The chicken should be at room temperature for cooking. If the meat is to be used in a casserole, appearance of the skin is not important. If the bird is to be served whole, it should be visually appealing. Cooked as is, the color will be a light golden tint. A more pleasing and appetizing look will be achieved if the bird is first patted dry with a paper towel and basted. Use a mixture of 1½ teaspoons melted butter and 1½ teaspoons Kitchen Bouquet. Goose feathers—the kind you buy, not pluck—are superb for basting as they easily get into all the tight spaces. For a crisp skin the chicken must be placed under the broiler of a conventional oven after it has finished cooking.

After the chicken is basted, it needs to be tied up with ordinary kitchen string. Secure the legs and wings close to the body to make it as much one solid mass as possible. The tips of the wings and legs and the breastbone area need to be shielded with a small amount of foil. The foil is removed after the first half of the cooking time.

The chicken is ready to be placed on a roasting rack set in a glass baking dish. Poultry under 6 pounds starts on its back and is not turned over during cooking. Remove juices that collect in

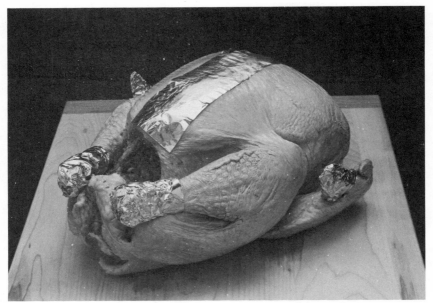

Thin areas of poultry—drumsticks, wing tips and breastbone—require shielding with small amounts of aluminum foil.

the dish during cooking with a basting tube. Reserve them in another bowl for making gravy later.

Do not use the temperature probe with poultry. The thickness of the meat varies too greatly for an accurate reading. The best test for doneness is the most basic. Wiggle a leg and if it is loose, rather than tight, it is done.

Allow a standing time for carry-over cooking. This also allows the juices to settle so that carving will be easier.

Chicken pieces cannot be fried in a microwave; leftovers can be reheated. Place the piece to be reheated on a dish lined with a paper towel to absorb moisture. Any chicken pieces coated with a crunchy mixture are cooked uncovered. A covering would hold in the steam and produce soggy, rather than crisp, chicken.

Chicken breasts are at their best when skinned and boned. With a sharp paring knife this is easy to do. Slip the tip of the knife between the edge of the bone and the meat. Keep the knife close to the bone and gently pull the meat away as you cut.

How the pieces are arranged in the dish is important. Thick portions go on the outer edge and thin portions toward the center. This allows all the pieces to cook equally. A tight covering of plastic wrap holds in the steam, prevents drying out, and aids in distributing the heat evenly.

Poultry to be cooked on a charcoal grill can be partially cooked in the microwave. It saves time and keeps the bird from drying out during prolonged cooking.

At a cooking class I asked who had done a turkey in the microwave. Only one small hand timidly came up, and we were all told how it had been done with great success—by a fourteen-year-old boy.

If you can roast a chicken, you can roast a turkey. The first step is to select the right turkey. Any size up to 16 pounds will do nicely. A larger turkey takes up so much space in the oven that the microwaves are not evenly distributed. Fresh is preferable to self-basting, although it cooks well, too. Self-basting turkeys have oil or a similar substance injected between the skin and the meat which may not be evenly distributed. Pop-up indicators do not function properly in the microwave and should be removed or disregarded.

One of the nicest favors you can do for yourself is to defrost the turkey in the microwave. Check the charts that came with your oven for exact times and settings. In general, a 10- to 12-pound turkey requires 30 minutes with the microwave and 30 minutes of standing time. This lessens the chance of bacteria developing and eliminates overcrowding and dripping in the refrigerator for one or two days. Shielding thin areas with foil is recommended, as when defrosting a chicken.

Stuffing a turkey does not increase the cooking time. Allow room for expansion when filling the cavity with dressing. The dressing will be moist, preventing the juices from running down your arms as you turn the turkey from breast to back.

After stuffing the turkey, pat it dry with a paper towel so the basting will adhere. Brush on 1 tablespoon of butter mixed with 1 tablespoon of bouquet sauce. Tie the legs and wings to the body and shield thin areas with foil. The foil over the breastbone should be secured with toothpicks.

Place the turkey on a roasting rack in a large glass baking dish. Allow 7 to 8 minutes per pound. The first half of the cooking time is on High, the second half at 70% power. Divide the total time into quarters. The turkey is breast down for the first quarter, breast up for the second quarter. The easiest way to turn the turkey is by hand, using folded paper towels to protect your

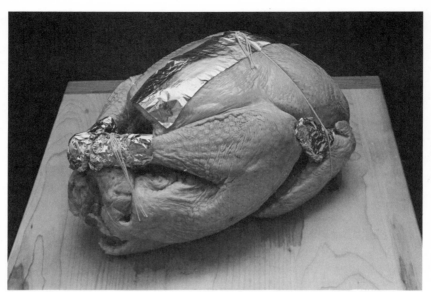

Tie the legs and wings close to the body for a more even density.

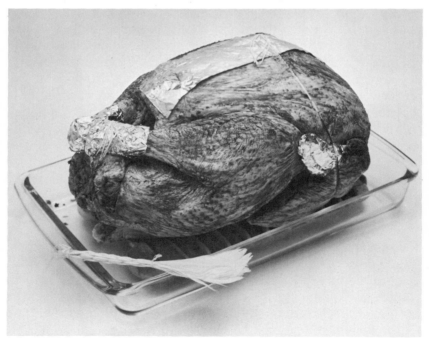

A basting mixture of butter and bouquet sauce applied with goose feathers is the finishing touch.

Microwaved poultry can be the most delicious, attractive and easiest ever prepared.

hands from the heat. At the halfway mark, remove the foil and the juices. Place the turkey on its breast for the third quarter of cooking time. The final quarter is on the back, and touch-up basting is done at this time. Allow a minimum of 15 minutes' standing time. For a 10-pound turkey, it takes 1 hour to thaw and 80 minutes to cook. No more getting up at the crack of dawn and going to bed exhausted that evening. Do the turkey in the microwave and enjoy the day along with everyone else.

Wild game is always cooked at 70% power. It is high in fat content and should be cooked on a rack with the juices drained frequently. The skin on a duck should be pricked all over to render the fat. The skin will not crisp, so if that is essential to the recipe it is best done conventionally. Quail is also best cooked conventionally due to its small size.

17. Eggs and Dairy Products

Preparing eggs in the microwave oven requires precise timing and a 70% power setting. The general rule is 30 seconds per egg. This may vary slightly due to size and age. Eggs should be slightly undercooked in the oven and allowed to finish during a brief standing time.

Scrambled eggs are more moist and have greater volume when compared to those cooked in a skillet. The trick is to stir them several times during cooking rather than once. If they are at all dry, cut back on the cooking time.

Poached eggs are a bit temperamental. The yolk has a higher fat content than the white and attracts more microwaves. The white may not set during cooking but will do so during the standing time. A small amount of vinegar added to the water helps the white coagulate. A tight covering holds in the steam and makes cooking more even. Pierce the membrane over the yolk to avoid a messy clean-up.

Fried eggs and *omeletes* are best done on a stove top. Whole eggs in the shell are not done in the microwave under any circumstances. To reheat a hard-cooked egg, it must be cut in half, even if the shell has been removed.

If one or two chopped, *hard-cooked eggs* are called for in a recipe, there is a quick and easy way to do it. Break the egg into a small cereal bowl and pierce the yolk in two or three places with a fork, being careful not to let the yolk run. Cover the bowl with plastic wrap. Cook at 50% power for 2 minutes for a large egg. (Time will vary according to the size of the egg and whether it is straight from the refrigerator or at room temperature.) Allow the egg to stand, covered, for 30 seconds to a minute to complete the cooking process. The egg will be firm and ready for chopping.

Cheese requires a 70% power setting. Rapid cooking on High turns it tough and rubbery. Cheese will melt best if it is grated. As a topping for a dish, cheese is added during the last one or two minutes of cooking time so that it will not become tough.

When baking *custard* it is not necessary to set the bowl in a container of water. Set the power anywhere from 30% to 50%.

Pies, quiches, and custards will cook through to the center if placed on top of an inverted dish. This allows more microwave penetration from underneath.

Use a large container to prevent boiling over, and no cover. Individual cups may be used but each will finish at a slightly different rate. To check for doneness, insert a knife in the center. If it comes out clean, the custard is ready.

A *pudding mix* cooks in 6 minutes on High. An individual serving can be made by combining 2 tablespoons of mix with ½ cup of milk. Cook on High for 1½ to 2 minutes. A *custard mix* takes 10 minutes on 70% power. For either, use a large, uncovered bowl and stir several times.

Sauces and *gravy* do well in the microwave oven and require less stirring than when prepared at the stove. Scorching is not a problem because the heat is spread evenly rather than being concentrated on the bottom. Sauces and gravy will continue to thicken during the standing time. Any lumps can be smoothed out in a blender or food processor.

Quiche will do best if the shell is baked first. Warm the milk or partially cook the filling before pouring it into the shell. It will cook through to the center if the quiche dish is placed on top of an inverted glass pie plate. This technique allows better microwave penetration from underneath.

18. Rice and Pastas

Rice and pastas take as long to cook in the microwave as on the stove. In the summer the kitchen will be cooler if they are prepared in the microwave. Otherwise, cook rice or pasta on the stove and use the microwave for another part of the meal.

Whichever appliance is used, there is a trick to keep pastas from sticking together: add a small amount of oil to the water. Pastas have no standing time and can be eaten immediately.

Rice must be cooked in a bowl large enough for it to expand to two or three times the original volume. The standing time is 5 minutes, covered. Always fluff rice with a fork. Rice that is stirred may be gummy. Rice does reheat nicely in the microwave. When converting a recipe, substitute quick-cooking for raw rice. The yield will be approximately one-third less since quick-cooking rice is partially rehydrated.

19. Fruits

For a true taste treat, prepare fruit in the microwave. It cooks very quickly on a High setting and retains its full flavor and shape. After making a batch of applesauce in minutes, you may never buy another can.

Fresh fruit cannot be dried in a microwave, but dried fruit can be rehydrated. Place a thin layer of dried fruit in a dish and barely cover with water, wine, or sherry. Tightly cover the dish and cook on High for about 5 minutes. Let it stand for 5 minutes to complete the process.

A fresh peach will peel more easily if it is placed in the oven for 10 seconds and allowed to stand for 5 minutes. Remember that a tomato dipped in boiling water just until the skin begins to split will peel very easily. Citrus fruits give more juice if they are first warmed for 15 seconds.

Fruit prepared in the microwave retains its fresh flavor and can be attractively cooked and served in natural shells.

20. Vegetables

The easiest and the best type of food to prepare in a microwave is vegetables. Easy because they can all be cooked on High (with the exception of the delicate mushroom). Best because little, if any, water is added. If water is not added, water is not poured off. The vegetables retain their nutrition, full flavor, shape, and color.

Canned vegetables have already been cooked. They may be reheated on 80% power or High. They heat more rapidly if most of the liquid is poured off before cooking. Stir partway into the cooking time. The liquid can be saved and added to soup stock for additional flavor and nutrition.

Frozen vegetables are not thawed before cooking. Those packaged in a paper—not foil—wrapped box can be cooked in the box. Liquid may leak onto the bottom of the oven but it is easier to wipe it up with a sponge than to wash a dirty bowl. After cooking, drain the vegetables by cutting a slit in one corner of the box.

Food packaged in a heat-sealed plastic bag can be cooked in the pouch. Again, no dirty dishes to clean. The pouch must have a slit made in the top to allow steam to escape during cooking.

Whenever possible, put the frozen food in icy side up. The water will drain over the food as it melts. When in doubt about how long to cook, follow the package instructions for the time given after water on the stove has reached a boil. If cooked in a bowl, add no water, cover tightly with plastic wrap, and stir partway into the cooking time.

Fresh vegetables are to microwave cooking what a star is to the top of a Christmas tree. If you grow your own in a small garden patch or on a full-fledged farm, you are indeed fortunate. If not, take advantage of seasonal produce in the supermarket or at the increasingly popular farmer's markets.

If a vegetable has been rinsed it may not be necessary to add water at all. For a softer, rather than crisp, vegetable, add 2 tablespoons of water per pound. For a real Southern-style vegetable even more water may be added but remember to increase the cooking time as well. Cover the dish tightly with plastic wrap and stir partway into the cooking time.

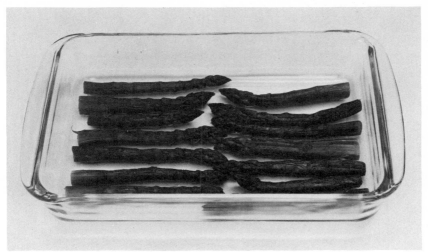

Protect the tender tips of asparagus by placing them in the center of the baking dish.

Do not sprinkle vegetables with salt. It can cause tough, dried spots and darken the color. Salt may be added to taste after cooking. If you absolutely cannot cook without salt, dissolve it in water before adding it to the vegetables.

The quality of the vegetables will affect the cooking time. The fresher vegetables contain more moisture and will cook more rapidly. If you chop the vegetables, make the pieces uniform in size for uniform cooking. A food processor is ideal for that chore.

Asparagus, broccoli, and cauliflower should be carefully arranged for even cooking. The stalks, which require longer cooking, go on the outer edge of the dish. Place the tender tips or flowerets to the center.

Potatoes and squash cooked in their skins must be pricked with a fork to allow for expansion. If the potato skins are too moist, place potatoes on a paper towel during cooking. Long potatoes will cook better than round potatoes. They may be prepared in advance. Wrapped in foil after being cooked, a potato retains its heat for 45 minutes.

Fresh corn can be cooked in the husk. If you think there might be a worm in it, pull the husk back, clean the ear, and pull the husk back in place and secure it with string. Frozen ears of corn are wrapped individually in waxed paper.

Corn may be cooked in the husk. If three or less are cooked at the same time, they may be placed in the oven as pictured.

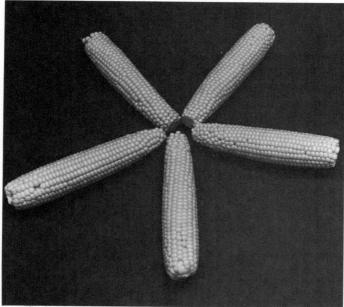

Shucked corn is wrapped in waxed paper for cooking. Four or more ears cooked at the same time are arranged like the spokes of a wheel. The thin end is toward the center and the thicker end on the outer edge.

Sauté onions, pepper, garlic, and mushrooms in the microwave. It is done quickly and it is necessary to stir only once. To cut calories, do not add butter to onions. They release enough moisture on their own to be tenderized.

Some vegetables require longer cooking than others. If they are to be combined, start one before adding the other. Do not mix canned vegetables with fresh or frozen at the beginning of a cooking time. Wait until the fresh or frozen are as tender as the canned product.

Here are some tips on how to select fresh vegetables.

ASPARAGUS: The stalks should be fairly straight and green, not yellow. The buds are dark and tightly closed. Snap, not cut, the ends of the stalks.

BEANS: Bend the pod in half to see if it is crisp enough to snap easily. Bulging pods may be tough.

BEETS: They should be medium size, smooth, and deep red.

BROCCOLI: The stalks should be firm. The buds are deep green and tightly closed in a compact cluster.

CABBAGE: The head should be solid and firm with no withered leaves.

CARROTS: They should be firm with good color and no green at the top. Small carrots have a better flavor.

CAULIFLOWER: Size does not affect flavor. The flowerets should be closely packed. Dark spots develop with age.

CORN: The husks should be green; dry husks show that corn is past its peak. Look for straight rows of kernels.

CUCUMBER: It should be firm, slender, and dark green.

EGGPLANT: It should be heavy and have firm flesh. Dull skin means it is past its prime.

LETTUCE: Judge by weight, not size. It should be heavy.

MUSHROOMS: They should be dry and firm. Look underneath to see if the cap is closed around the stem; it spreads with age. Do not wash mushrooms; wipe the caps with a damp paper towel. Do not pull out the stems; cut so that some stem remains in the center to hold a better shape.

ONIONS: They should be firm with dry skin and no sprouts. To peel, let stand 1 minute in boiling water. Rub hands with lemon juice to remove odor.

PEAS: The pods should be bright green. Add a pinch of sugar to emphasize their sweet flavor.

Vegetables chopped in uneven sizes will cook unevenly.

Chop, dice and slice uniformly because each piece cooks individually.

PEPPERS: The color should be bright and the flesh thick. Red peppers are the same as green, only more mature.

POTATO: It should be firm and well shaped with no cracks, sprouts, or dark, soft spots.

SPINACH: It should have large, fresh leaves that are dark green.

SQUASH: Winter: It should be firm and heavy for its size. It may be smooth or bumpy. Summer: It should be small and heavy for its size. The rind should be shiny and soft enough to yield to slight pressure.

SWEET POTATO: The size should be small to medium and tapered at each end.

TOMATO: It should be firm with no soft spots. If not for immediate use, purchase slightly underripe. To peel, let stand in boiling water about 1 minute or until skin begins to crack.

TURNIP: It should be firm and heavy for its size. The skin should be smooth.

21. Cakes, Quick Breads, Pastries

You can bake in the microwave, but baking does require some special techniques. First of all, cakes do not brown unless their ingredients, such as chocolate, give them some color. Since cakes are usually frosted or have a topping, this is really no problem. Neither do they form a crust. For that reason, they rise higher and are very tender and moist. The two types of cakes which are not recommended for a microwave are angel food and pound cake.

For a level cake, mix the batter by hand and allow it to stand at room temperature for 10 minutes. If the cake has a bitter taste, reduce the amount of the leavening agent the next time you use the recipe. If the center cannot be finished without overcooking the edges, reduce the liquid. Cakes that are high in fat content will bake more rapidly.

Always use a round container as corners tend to overcook. Glass or hard plastic cake dishes, bundt pans, and ring molds are

Microwaved cakes tend to be a bit wavy on the surface. This characteristic can be minimized if the proper steps are followed in preparation. The cake is done if it is pulling away from the edge of the dish.

most often used. Do not grease and flour the dish. If the cake or bread is to be sliced in the dish, no greasing is necessary. If it is to be turned out, line the bottom of the dish with waxed paper. Cut several liners at one time and store them with the dishes so that they will always be handy.

Because microwave-baked cakes do rise higher, fill the container halfway. Otherwise, you will have a spillover. Bake one layer at a time. The layers will be more level if baked individually. Standard baking time is 6 to 7 minutes at 60% power and 3 minutes on High. Extra batter can be used for cupcakes. One cupcake bakes on High for 30 seconds.

At the end of the baking time, the cake should still be moist on top. If it is pulling away from the edge of the dish at any one spot, do not put it back in the oven. Let it stand on a flat surface for 5 minutes. Excess moisture can be blotted with a paper towel. If the center is still soupy, cook a little longer.

Frosting the cake can literally be a crummy job since there is no crust. To eliminate this problem, completely cool or chill the cake. Spread the frosting while it is still warm or at room temperature.

Keep cakes and quick breads in an airtight container. They are very moist but, without a crust, will dry out quickly unless carefully stored.

Pie pastry can be baked in the microwave and will be very flaky. It will not brown. Pie shells should be pre-baked and completely cooled before filling. Crumb crusts bake beautifully and are a good alternative to pastry shells. Be sure the sugar is well mixed with the crumbs. A clump of sugar will overcook. If that does happen, simply lift out the burned spot. The burned flavor does not spread to the rest of the crust. Cream-filled chocolate cookies can be used for crusts in place of chocolate wafers. Just omit the sugar since the filling supplies the sweetness.

22. Cookies and Candy

Cookies are best made in a conventional oven. In the microwave they will neither brown nor crust. So few can be done at one time that it may actually take longer. Chocolate chip cookies are unsuitable because the microwaves are strongly attracted to the high sugar concentration of the chips. The result is overcooked chips and doughy cookie.

Making candy in the microwave eliminates the use of a double boiler. It is a superb method for melting chocolate. Real chocolate is recommended since artificial chocolate contains extra fats which melt rapidly and tend to separate. If melting is judged by the chocolate running, it will be ruined. Chocolate chips retain their shape until stirred. Chocolate squares can be melted in the wrapper and simply scraped off the paper into the waiting mixture. Fifty percent is the power setting for melting chocolate.

Candy syrups that must reach a certain temperature on a candy thermometer are a bit tricky to achieve. The microwave temperature probe does not have high enough readings to be used. Currently an effort is under way to perfect a candy thermometer for microwave cooking. Until it is available, rely on the water test.

THREAD: A small quantity dropped into ice water forms a soft thread. 230°–234°

SOFT BALL: A small quantity dropped into ice water forms a ball. The ball will flatten out when picked up with the fingers. 234°–240°

FIRM BALL: A small quantity dropped into ice water will form a ball that holds its shape unless pressed with the fingers. 242°–248°

HARD BALL: A small quantity dropped into ice water will form a ball that holds its shape but is still pliable. 250°–268°

SOFT CRACK: A small quantity dropped into ice water will separate into hard threads. When removed from the water they are not brittle. 270°–288°

HARD CRACK: A small quantity dropped into ice water will separate into hard threads that remain brittle. 290°–310°

23. Recipe Conversion

The preceding sections have given most of what you need to know for converting recipes from conventional instructions to a microwave oven. Here are a few additional tips to keep in mind.

1. Most, but not all, recipes convert successfully. If a crust or crunchiness is essential to the finished dish, the dry heat of a conventional oven is necessary. Soufflés, angel food cake, and popovers do not convert well because they require dry heat. Yeast bread can be done quickly but will not have a crust. Are you willing to exchange "crunch" for the time saved?
2. Compare the conventional recipe to a microwave recipe with similar ingredients. What power settings are used? Is the dish covered? Adjust the time according to the quantity. If the conventional recipe calls for 2 pounds of meat and the similar microwave recipe uses only 1 pound, you will need to almost double the microwave time.
3. If you cannot find a similar recipe, allow approximately one-fourth the time required in the conventional recipe. If the ingredients include cheese, eggs, cream, pork, or lamb, a 70% power setting is required.
4. Simmering is done at 50% power for about the same amount of time as required conventionally to allow flavors to blend.
5. It is rarely necessary to grease a dish. There is no dry heat to bake the food onto the dish.
6. Liquid content is usually reduced since there is less evaporation during cooking.
7. Remember to stir at intervals to redistribute the food for even cooking.
8. Go easy on the seasonings. Flavors are more pronounced in microwave cooking. If at the end of cooking the taste is too subtle more spices can be added.
9. Allow for additional cooking to occur during the standing time.

The most important thing to remember is to be conservative in estimating the time it will take a dish to cook. Microwave cooking is fast so don't overdo it! A dish that is undercooked can be put back in the oven. A dish that is overcooked will probably be thrown out.

Have fun with it! Relax and realize that, once upon a time, cooks had to conquer those newfangled stoves that replaced the old wood burners. They did . . . and so will you.

WHAT'S COOKING?

BREAKFAST

Granola

4 cups rolled oats
1 cup sunflower seeds
½ cup slivered almonds
½ cup cashew pieces
¼ cup shredded coconut
½ cup wheat germ
2 tablespoons nonfat powdered milk
½ cup vegetable oil
¼ cup honey
1 tablespoon vanilla
½ to 1 cup brown sugar
1 cup raisins or chopped dried apples

1. Combine oats, sunflower seeds, almonds, cashews, coconut, wheat germ, and powdered milk in a very large bowl and mix well.

2. In a 1-cup measure, combine oil, honey, and vanilla. Pour over the granola. It is important to stir well and be sure the entire mixture is evenly coated or there will be spots that overcook.

3. Cook on High for 8 minutes, stirring every 2 minutes.

4. Add brown sugar and fruit.

5. Cool, stirring occasionally. Cooling will be faster if mixture is spread out on a cookie sheet.

6. Store in an airtight container.

Uncle Jim's Egg Muffins

SERVES 2

2 eggs, fried
2 slices cooked ham
2 slices American cheese
1 English muffin, split and toasted

1. Place an egg on top of each muffin half; add a slice of ham; top with a piece of cheese.
2. Place muffin halves on top of a paper towel in a serving dish. Heat in oven at 70% power for 30 seconds to 1 minute or until cheese has melted.
3. Remove paper towel and serve hot.

Festival Egg Ring

SERVES 6

6 eggs, beaten
¼ cup milk
½ teaspoon salt
¼ teaspoon pepper
10 stuffed olives, sliced
2 tablespoons butter or margarine, melted
1 tomato, peeled, and chopped
½ cup shredded Cheddar cheese

1. Combine all ingredients and mix well.
2. Pour mixture into a ring mold.
3. Bake at 70% power for 8 to 10 minutes, rotating dish twice.
4. Let stand for about 2 minutes before serving.

Brunch Egg Ring

¼ cup butter or margarine, melted
1½ dozen eggs, beaten
1 cup sour cream
¾ cup milk
2 teaspoons salt
1 teaspoon freeze-dried chives
¼ teaspoon tarragon
  pinch of cayenne pepper
  paprika
  parsley
  tomatoes, sliced
  bacon, cooked

1. In a large bowl combine butter, eggs, sour cream, milk, salt, chives, tarragon (crushed to release flavor), and cayenne pepper. Blend well, by hand.

2. Lightly grease a microwave bundt pan.

3. Pour egg mixture into bundt pan and bake at 70% power for 16 to 20 minutes. It is important to rotate the dish four or five times during the cooking period.

4. Let stand for about 2 minutes.

5. Turn the egg ring out onto a serving plate. Sprinkle the top lightly with paprika to add color. Garnish with parsley, tomato slices, and cooked bacon.

Pancakes Deluxe

Pancakes are prepared by conventional methods. The trick is to make extra so that they can be stored in a plastic bag in the refrigerator or freezer and reheated in the microwave as needed.

1 cup flour
2 tablespoons sugar
2 teaspoons baking powder
½ teaspoon salt
1 cup milk
1 egg
2 tablespoons oil
1 large banana, sliced thin
¼ cup chopped pecans or walnuts

1. Combine flour, sugar, baking powder, and salt and set aside.
2. Blend together milk, egg, and oil. Stir in dry ingredients.
3. Stir in bananas and nuts.
4. Cook on a greased griddle until lightly browned.

The first two steps can be done the night before and the batter refrigerated. All you need do the next morning is add the banana and nuts.

To reheat the pancakes, place them on a serving plate, spread with butter, top with syrup and heat on High for about 45 seconds for two pancakes.

Top to bottom:
Granola (p. 51). Instant Russian Tea (p. 68). Uncle Jim's Egg Muffins (p. 52).

Banana Smash

For those mornings when even a microwave oven is not fast enough!

2 bananas, peeled and broken into chunks
1 cup grapefruit juice
1 cup orange juice
1 cup milk
2 tablespoons honey
1 teaspoon vanilla

1. Combine all ingredients in a blender. Process until smooth.
2. Chill until time to serve.

Top to bottom:
Gerry's Dip (p. 62). Cashew-Mushroom Canapes (p. 60). Deviled Mushroom Caps (p. 59).

Appetizers and Snacks

Crystallized Orange Pecans

YIELD: 2 CUPS

¼ cup orange juice
1 cup sugar
2 cups pecan halves

1. In a 1½-quart bowl, combine orange juice and sugar. Add pecans. Cook at 70% power for 6 minutes, stir, cook 8 to 10 minutes more. Syrup should be crystallized.
2. Spread and separate glazed nuts on greased cookie sheet. Cool completely. Store in an airtight container.

Aloha Spread

YIELD: ABOUT 1½ CUPS

1 (6¾-ounce) can chicken meat, flaked
3 slices bacon, cooked and crumbled
½ cup drained crushed pineapple
¼ cup chopped walnuts or pecans
1 tablespoon soy or teriyaki sauce
   salty crackers

1. Combine all ingredients, except crackers, in a small bowl. This can be done ahead of time and stored in the refrigerator.
2. Spread a small portion on each cracker. Arrange crackers on a microwave-safe platter and warm in the oven before serving. A High setting is used. Time will vary according to how many are being done.

Sweet and Sour Chicken Wings

YIELD: 16

1 ½ pounds chicken wings
  oil
  salt
  cornstarch
1 egg, beaten

Sauce:

⅛ cup soy sauce
¼ cup vinegar
¼ cup sugar
1 ½ tablespoons catsup
½ teaspoon salt
¼ cup apple jelly
1 teaspoon lemon juice

1. Cut the tips from wings and discard. Cut apart at the joint.
2. Pour enough oil in a frying pan to coat the bottom. Heat the oil.
3. Lightly salt each piece, coat with cornstarch, and dip in beaten egg.
4. Fry on top of the stove until golden brown. Drain on a paper towel.
5. Combine all ingredients for the sauce in a bowl. Bring to a boil on High. Stir to blend well.
6. Pour sauce over wings and simmer in microwave oven for 10 minutes at 50% power.
7. Place on serving platter or keep warm in chafing dish.

Mushroom Caviar

YIELD: ABOUT ¾ CUP

1 small onion, chopped fine
1 tablespoon butter
½ pound mushrooms
1 teaspoon salt
¼ teaspoon pepper
1 tablespoon Worcestershire sauce
1 tablespoon mayonnaise
    fresh parsley sprigs
    thin wheat crackers

1. Sauté the onions in butter on High for 2 minutes, stirring once.
2. Clean the mushrooms with a damp paper towel. Cut off the tough end of the stem. Dice extremely fine or process in a food processor (stems as well as caps).
3. Add mushrooms to onions and sauté on High for 1½ minutes.
4. Stir in remaining ingredients.
5. Place in a fine mesh strainer to drain excess liquid.
6. Shape in a mound on a serving dish and chill.
7. Garnish with a ring of fresh parsley and a circle of thin wheat crackers around the mound.

Mushrooms in Barbecue Sauce

½ cup butter or margarine, melted
1 cup catsup
¼ cup red wine vinegar
¼ cup lemon juice
2 tablespoons Worcestershire sauce
2 tablespoons dark brown sugar
1 tablespoon prepared mustard
1 tablespoon dried minced onion
    dash of hot sauce
1 pound fresh mushrooms
2 tablespoons butter or margarine

1. Combine all ingredients, except mushrooms and 2 tablespoons butter, in a round bowl. Simmer at 50% power for 10 minutes.

2. Sauté mushrooms in 2 tablespoons butter, covered, at 70% power for 2 minutes, stirring once.

3. Combine mushrooms and sauce in a chafing dish; serve warm.

Deviled Mushroom Caps

2   pounds large, fresh mushrooms
4   tablespoons butter
1   (4½-ounce) can deviled ham
¼   cup sour cream
1½ teaspoons dried chives
     stuffed green olives

1. Clean the mushrooms by wiping the cap with a damp paper towel. Break off the stems but reserve enough to make ½ cup when chopped.

2. Work with 1 pound of mushrooms at a time.

3. Melt 2 tablespoons of butter in a glass pie plate. Add mushrooms and sauté, uncovered, at 70% power for 3 to 4 minutes, stirring once. Repeat with second pound of mushrooms.

4. Chop very fine enough stems to equal ½ cup. Add deviled ham, sour cream, and chopped chives. Blend well.

5. Again, work with half the mushrooms at a time. Arrange them on a platter, preferably round, and stuff each one with the ham mixture. Garnish the top with a slice of olive. Reheat at 70% power for about 2 minutes or until all are warm. Repeat with second half. Serve warm.

Cashew-Mushroom Canapés

1 pound large, fresh mushrooms
2 tablespoons butter, melted
¾ cup fine-chopped mushroom stems
1 tablespoon dried minced onion
1½ teaspoons dried parsley, minced
   pinch of dill
1 slice white bread, crumbed
1 tablespoon butter, melted
½ cup cashews, ground or fine-chopped
   whole cashews

1. Clean the mushrooms by wiping them with a damp paper towel. Break off the stems but reserve enough to equal ¾ cup when chopped. Brush each cap with melted butter. Arrange, bottoms up, on a platter, preferably round.

2. Combine chopped stems, onion, parsley, dill (crushed between fingers to release flavor), bread crumbs, 1 tablespoon melted butter, and ground cashews. Fill the center of each mushroom cap with the mixture. Top with a whole cashew.

3. Heat at 70% power for 5 to 7 minutes, rotating dish once. Serve hot.

Swiss Cheese Fondue

SERVES 4

1 pound Swiss cheese, shredded
1 small garlic clove, pressed
2 cups dry white wine
1 teaspoon dry mustard
¼ teaspoon salt
⅛ teaspoon white pepper
2 tablespoons cornstarch
2 tablespoons water
1 tablespoon lemon juice
1 loaf French bread, cut into bite-size cubes

1. In a 3-quart bowl combine the Swiss cheese, garlic, wine, mustard, salt, and pepper. Cook, uncovered, at 70% power for 10 to 12 minutes, stirring every 3 minutes. The cheese will not look as if it is melting properly until very near the end of the cooking time.

2. Use a small bowl to combine the cornstarch with the water and lemon juice. Stir out all the lumps. Add to the cheese mixture and blend well.

3. Cook for 1 to 2 minutes on High or until cheese just begins to boil. Boil for 1 minute.

4. Serve in a fondue pot or in a glass bowl, with the bread cubes at hand for dipping. Reheat the fondue at 70% power briefly when the cheese begins to cool.

Cream Cheese Spread

YIELD: ABOUT ¾ CUP

1 (8-ounce) package cream cheese
2 slices bacon
  peel of 1 orange, grated
  melba toast

1. Soften cream cheese.
2. Cook bacon on High for 2 to 3 minutes. Crumble it or dice it fine.
3. Combine cream cheese and bacon. Add orange peel.
4. Allow to set for at least 1 hour to blend flavors.
5. Serve at room temperature with melba toast.

Curried Cheese Spread

YIELD: ABOUT 1½ CUPS

8 ounces sharp Cheddar cheese, shredded
½ to ¾ cup mayonnaise
30 stuffed green olives, chopped fine
½ teaspoon curry powder
  sliced olives for garnish
  thin wheat crackers

1. In a medium-size bowl, combine the cheese, mayonnaise, chopped olives, and curry powder.

2. Place about ⅓ teaspoon of cheese mixture on each cracker and top with an olive slice. If too much cheese is used it will melt off the cracker. Place in oven at 70% power and bake just long enough to melt the cheese. It will probably take about 5 seconds per cracker but the exact time will depend on how many are being heated.

Parmesan Canapés

YIELD: 2 DOZEN

3 slices bacon
½ cup grated Parmesan cheese
¼ cup half-and-half
½ teaspoon Worcestershire sauce
⅛ teaspoon cayenne pepper or paprika
   pimiento-stuffed olives, sliced
24 small toast rounds

1. Cook bacon on High for 3 to 4 minutes.

2. Crumble bacon and combine with cheese, half-and-half, Worcestershire sauce, and cayenne.

3. Spread cheese mixture on each toast round and top with an olive slice.

4. Cover bottom of a platter with paper toweling to absorb the moisture and arrange the canapés on it. Use a 70% power setting and allow approximately 10 seconds per canapé.

5. Serve hot.

Gerry's Dip

YIELD: ABOUT 3 CUPS

1 cup Parmesan cheese
1 cup mayonnaise
1 (14-ounce) can artichoke hearts, drained and chopped
   paprika

1. Combine cheese, mayonnaise, and artichokes in a 1- or 1½-quart bowl.
2. Cook at 70% power for 4 minutes, stirring after 2 minutes.
3. Sprinkle top with paprika.
4. Serve hot with thin wheat crackers.
5. If dip cools, reheat at 70% power. Time will depend on how much is left.

Smoked Beef Dip

YIELD: 2½ CUPS

1   package smoked beef, chopped fine
8   ounces cream cheese, softened
½ cup sour cream
1   small onion, minced
¼ green pepper, minced
1   small celery stalk, minced
1   tablespoon milk
½ cup chopped walnuts or ½ cup chopped olives

1. Combine all ingredients in a bowl.
2. Heat at 70% power for 2 to 4 minutes, stirring every minute. Just warm, do not melt.
3. Serve warm with crackers or chips.

Crab Florentine

YIELD: ABOUT 3 CUPS

2 (10-ounce) packages frozen chopped spinach, cooked
½ cup butter or margarine
½ cup thin-sliced green onions
1 garlic clove, pressed
1 cup grated Parmesan cheese
1 (6½-ounce) can crabmeat
   melba toast, bland crackers, or pumpernickel

1. After the spinach is cooked, place it in a colander to drain while you continue with the recipe.

2. In a 2- or 3-quart bowl, place the butter, onions, and garlic. Cook, uncovered, on High for 1 to 1½ minutes, just long enough for the butter to melt.

3. Stir in the drained spinach and cheese.

4. Carefully remove any small bits of shell that may be in the crabmeat. Stir crab into spinach. Warm at 70% power for 1 to 2 minutes before placing in a small chafing dish.

5. Serve with melba toast, crackers, or pumpernickle. Crab Florentine would also be tasty as a crepe filling.

Beverages

Brown Bear Broth

YIELD: 8 SIX-OUNCE SERVINGS

2   (10½-ounce) cans beef broth or
2½ cups beef bouillon
2   cups (dry) burgundy wine
1   cup hot water
10 whole cloves
    small pinch of cayenne pepper

1. Combine all ingredients in a pitcher or large bowl.
2. Heat, uncovered, on High for 6 minutes. Stir. Lower power to 50% and simmer for 5 minutes.
3. Best served steaming hot on a cold, snowy evening.

Spiced Tomato Juice

SERVES 4 TO 6

1 (18-ounce) can tomato juice
1 can beef broth
¼ cup lemon juice
1 teaspoon horseradish
1 teaspoon dried parsley flakes
½ teaspoon celery salt
2 tablespoons dry sherry, optional

1. Combine all ingredients, except sherry, in a 4-cup measure. Cook on High for 8 minutes, stirring once, or until heated through.
2. Stir in sherry if desired.

Mulled Cider

SERVES 12

8 cups (2 quarts) apple cider
½ cup brown sugar, packed firm
12 whole cloves
2 cinnamon sticks

1. Combine all ingredients in a large bowl. Cook on High for 14 minutes or until temperature probe reads 160°.
2. Strain and serve in mugs or cups.

Mulled Wine

SERVES 12

4 cups (1 quart) burgundy wine
   peel of 1 orange
   peel of 1 lemon
1 stick cinnamon
6 whole cloves
1 dash of nutmeg
1 tablespoon sugar

1. Combine all ingredients in a large bowl and cook at 50% power for 5 to 8 minutes.
2. Strain and serve in 4 ounce wine glass.

Dessert Chocolate

SERVES 4

1 cup semisweet chocolate bits
2 tablespoons instant coffee
1 cup water
1 teaspoon vanilla
½ teaspoon ground cinnamon
4 cups milk
   whipped cream, optional

1. Combine chocolate, coffee, and water in a large bowl. Cook on High for 3 to 4 minutes. The chocolate will not be completely melted.

2. Add vanilla, cinnamon, and milk; blend well. Cook on High for 6 minutes.

3. Serve hot, topped with whipped cream.

Quick Irish Coffee

SERVES 2

¼ to ½ cup Irish whiskey
3 to 4 tablespoons sugar
2 tablespoons instant coffee
2 cups hot water
  whipped cream

1. Combine all ingredients, except whipped cream, in a 4-cup measure or bowl; stir. Cook on High for 3 to 4 minutes. Do not boil. Stir to dissolve sugar.

2. Pour into mugs, stemmed glasses or coffee cups and top with whipped cream. Be sure cream is very stiff so that it will not blend with the coffee.

Coffee-Flavored Liqueur

YIELD: ABOUT 1½ QUARTS

3 cups sugar
2 cups water
6 tablespoons instant coffee (not freeze-dried)
1 pint brandy
1 vanilla bean, split
8 ounces vodka

1. In a large bowl, combine sugar and water; bring to a boil. Stir in coffee.

2. Cool to room temperature and add brandy and vanilla bean. Pour into a half-gallon jug. Shake well once a day for 30 days.

3. Add vodka.

4. Strain mixture through cheesecloth.

5. Pour into clean container. Store at room temperature.

Instant Russian Tea

½ to ¾ cup instant tea
1¼ cups sugar
2 cups orange breakfast drink powder
½ teaspoon ground cloves
1 teaspoon ground cinnamon
2 (3-ounce) packages lemonade mix

1. Combine all ingredients and store in an airtight container.

2. Use 2½ teaspoons per cup of boiling water.

Soup

Asparagus Cream Soup

SERVES 4

3 tablespoons butter
½ cup chopped onion
½ cup chopped celery
1 pound asparagus, cut in 1-inch pieces
   dash of curry powder
2 (13¾-ounce) cans chicken broth
   seasoned salt to taste
½ pint heavy cream
   chopped chives or parsley for garnish

1. In a large bowl, sauté onion and celery in butter, covered, until soft, about 2 to 3 minutes.
2. Stir in asparagus and curry powder. Stir in chicken broth and seasoned salt. Cover; cook on High for 8 minutes, stirring once or twice.
3. Add cream. Reduce power to 50% and cook, covered, for 20 minutes, stirring every 5 minutes. Do not boil.
4. Cool slightly. Pour into blender and blend until smooth. Process only half the mixture at a time and use a potholder to hold the blender top in place.
5. Strain mixture through a sieve to remove any strings.
6. Pour into individual bowls and garnish.

Corn Soup

SERVES 6

2 (10½-ounce) cans corn, drained
4 cups chicken broth (2 (13¾-ounce) cans plus water)
½ cup okra, chopped
1 garlic clove, chopped
½ cup chopped celery
1 cup diced cooked chicken
1 tablespoon butter or margarine
¾ teaspoon salt
¼ to ½ teaspoon pepper
2 cups milk

Combine all ingredients in a very large bowl. Cook, covered, at 80% power for 15 minutes, stirring every 5 minutes.

Chilled Cucumber Soup

SERVES 6

1 small onion, chopped
1 tablespoon butter
1 large cucumber, peeled, seeded, and sliced
2 (14½-ounce) cans chicken broth
¾ teaspoon dill weed
1½ teaspoons gelatin
¼ cup cold water
1 cup sour cream
¼ teaspoon salt
⅛ teaspoon white pepper

1. In a 3-quart bowl, sauté the onion in butter on High for 2 minutes, stirring once.
2. To seed the cucumber, try using a grapefruit spoon.
3. Add the sliced cucumber to the onions, cover tightly with plastic wrap, and cook on High for 1 minute, stirring once.
4. Pour the two cans of broth into a 4-cup measure and bring to a boil on High, stirring once. It will take about 6 minutes.

5. Stir dill weed and broth into bowl, cover, and cook on High for 8 to 10 minutes, stirring once. Cucumbers should be tender.

6. Dissolve gelatin in cold water. Stir into broth.

7. Allow broth to cool to lukewarm.

8. Stir in sour cream and blend with a whisk.

9. Purée mixture in a blender. If done in a food processor, work with half the amount at a time.

10. Pour back into the 3-quart bowl through a strainer. Use a wooden spoon to gently press the liquid from the purée.

11. Stir in salt and pepper.

12. Chill completely before serving. Garnish with fresh dill or crisp cucumber slices.

French Onion Soup

SERVES 4 TO 6

4 tablespoons butter, melted
2 large yellow onions, sliced
4 cups beef broth or 3 (10½-ounce) cans beef broth
½ teaspoon sugar
   pepper
½ cup dry sherry, optional
4 slices French bread, toasted
   grated Parmesan or Swiss cheese

1. In a deep bowl, sauté onions in butter on High for 5 minutes, covered, stirring once.

2. Stir in sugar and cook, uncovered, on High for 30 seconds.

3. Stir in beef broth and dash of pepper and simmer at 50% power, covered, for 15 minutes.

4. Add sherry if desired.

5. Pour into individual crocks or bowls.

6. Top with slice of bread and generous amount of grated cheese. Place in oven at 70% power just long enough to melt cheese.

Mushroom Soup

SERVES 6 TO 8

1 pound fresh mushrooms
6 tablespoons butter
4 tablespoons flour
2 (13¾-ounce) cans chicken broth
1 cup cream
1 cup milk
¼ cup sherry
   salt and white pepper to taste

1. Slice the mushrooms and chop the stems. Place in a 3-quart bowl with the butter and sauté on High for 1½ minutes. Stir to finish melting the butter and coating all the mushroom pieces. Sauté for another 1½ minutes.

2. Sprinkle flour on top of mushrooms and stir until it is absorbed.

3. Pour in chicken broth and stir. Cover and cook on High for 8 minutes, stirring once.

4. Simmer at 50% power, covered, for 10 to 12 minutes.

5. Gradually stir in milk, cream, and sherry.

6. Add salt and pepper to taste.

7. If the soup is reheated, use 50% power.

Cream of Tomato Soup

SERVES 4 TO 6

3 large or 4 medium-size tomatoes
2 tablespoons brown sugar
½ cup butter or margarine, melted
½ cup fiour
2 cups milk
2 teaspoons salt
   dash of hot sauce

1. Peel tomatoes and liquefy them in a blender or food processor.

2. Strain through a sieve.

3. Add brown sugar to tomato juice and cook, covered, on High for 3 minutes.

4. Stir flour into melted butter. Gradually add milk, stirring until sauce is smooth. Cook on High for 8 minutes, stirring every 2 minutes. If there are any lumps, use a wire whisk or blender to smooth the mixture.

5. Combine all ingredients, add hot sauce to taste, and heat through.

6. Do not allow mixture to boil.

Hot or Cold Tomato Soup

SERVES 10

12 large tomatoes
1 onion, chopped
1½ cups sour cream
1 tablespoon salt
2 teaspoons sugar
½ teaspoon thyme
½ teaspoon tarragon
¼ teaspoon cayenne pepper
2 tablespoons lime juice

1. Peel and quarter the tomatoes. Add onion and purée in a blender or food processor. Don't try to do all of them at one time.

2. Blend remaining ingredients in blender or processor.

3. Stir sour cream sauce and tomatoes together in a very large bowl. Simmer at 50% power for 12 to 14 minutes or until heated through.

4. Serve warm or chilled.

Greek Lemon Soup

SERVES 4

2 (13¾-ounce) cans chicken broth
2 tablespoons raw rice
  peel of 1 lemon, grated
2 tablespoons lemon juice
1 egg, beaten
1 lemon, sliced thin
  snipped parsley

1. In a 3-quart bowl, combine chicken broth and rice. Cook, covered, on High for 12 to 14 minutes, stirring every 4 minutes.
2. Combine lemon rind, lemon juice, and egg. Pour small amounts of hot liquid into egg mixture, stirring constantly. Add to broth. Continue cooking, covered, at 50% power for 5 to 6 minutes. Do not boil.
3. Serve immediately garnished with parsley and a lemon slice.

Chicken Noodle Soup

6 chicken bouillon cubes
6 cups hot water
1 cup chopped cooked chicken
4 ounces spaghetti, broken and cooked
  salt
  pepper

SERVES 4

1. Combine bouillon cubes and water. Bring to a boil, about 10 to 13 minutes. Stir to finish dissolving bouillon.
2. Combine all ingredients. Go easy on the salt and pepper.
3. Simmer, covered, at 50% power for 10 to 15 minutes.

Beefy Vegetable Soup

SERVES 4 TO 6

½ to ¾ pound round tip (sirloin tip) beef, cut into small pieces
  oil
1 (10½-ounce) can beef broth or 1¼ cups beef bouillon
1 (14½-ounce) can tomatoes, quartered
2 (8-ounce) cans tomato sauce
1 cup hot water
1 (16-ounce) package frozen mixed vegetables
½ cup alphabet macaroni
½ teaspoon salt
¼ teaspoon pepper
1 teaspoon sugar

1. Pour a small amount of oil into a skillet and, on the stove, brown the meat.

2. Combine all the ingredients, including drippings the meat browned in and liquid from the tomatoes, in a large bowl. Cover tightly with plastic wrap and cook on High for 6 to 8 minutes, stirring once.

3. Reduce power to 50% and simmer for 20 minutes, stirring every 5 minutes.

Corned Beef and Cabbage Chowder

SERVES 4 TO 6

2 tablespoons cornstarch
½ teaspoon salt
¼ teaspoon pepper
2 cups milk
¼ cup butter or margarine
2 celery stalks, chopped
½ green pepper, chopped
2 garlic cloves, pressed
2 cups chicken bouillon
2 carrots, scraped and sliced thin
5 ounces packaged sliced corned beef (for sandwiches)
2 cups shredded cabbage

1. In a 3-quart bowl, combine the cornstarch, salt, and pepper. Gradually stir in the milk and blend until all lumps are dissolved. Bring to a boil on High, about 4 minutes, stirring once. Stir out lumps quickly and boil for 1 minute. The sauce should be slightly thickened.

2. Sauté the celery and green pepper in butter on High for 3 minutes, stirring once. Add to the sauce.

3. Add the garlic, chicken bouillon, and carrots to the milk.

4. Cut the corned beef into thin strips and add to the milk. Cover and cook at 50% power for 12 to 16 minutes, stirring once.

5. Stir in cabbage and cook, uncovered, at 50% power for 3 minutes.

Breads

Croutons

6 cups bread cubes
½ cup butter or margarine, melted
    seasonings of your choice, such as ½ teaspoon garlic salt
      and 2 tablespoons Italian herb seasoning

1. In a large baking dish, spread bread cubes out evenly. Cook on High for 6 minutes, stirring every 2 minutes.
2. In a plastic bag, combine bread cubes, melted butter, and seasonings. Shake bag to coat bread cubes with butter and seasonings.
3. Pour back into the dish and cook on High for 4 to 6 minutes, stirring every minute until crisp.
4. Store in an airtight container.

Quick and Easy Cheese Bites

SERVES 6

1 (8-ounce) can refrigerator biscuits
¾ cup grated Parmesan cheese
½ teaspoon paprika
⅛ teaspoon garlic powder
1 tablespoon sesame seeds, optional
3 tablespoons butter or margarine, melted

1. Cut each biscuit in half to form a semicircle. For use as an appetizer they can be quartered.
2. In a small bowl combine cheese, paprika, garlic powder, and sesame seeds. Mix well.
3. Dip each biscuit piece in butter and roll in cheese mixture.

4. Arrange biscuits around edge of round cake pan and place an inverted glass in the center or use a ring mold.

5. Cook at 70% power for 4 to 6 minutes, rotating dish after 2 minutes. Repeat with second batch.

6. Serve warm.

Apple Surprise Coffee Cake

SERVES 6 TO 8

Topping:
4   tablespoons butter or margarine
½   cup dark brown sugar
¼   to ½ cup ground walnuts
⅛   teaspoon ground cinnamon
1   apple

Cake:
4   tablespoons butter or margarine
1   egg, beaten
½   cup milk
½   cup sugar
1   cup all-purpose flour
½   teaspoon salt
1½ teaspoons baking powder
¼   teaspoon ground cinnamon

1. Melt 4 tablespoons butter in bottom of round cake dish. Add ½ cup brown sugar, walnuts, and cinnamon and blend well.

2. Peel and slice the apple thin; arrange slices attractively on top of brown sugar mixture.

3. Melt 4 tablespoons butter in 2-cup measuring glass; stir in egg and milk.

4. In medium-size bowl combine sugar, flour, salt, baking powder, and cinnamon.

5. Combine liquid and dry ingredients, stirring just long enough to smooth out lumps. Pour on top of apples. Cook at 60% power for 6 to 7 minutes, rotating dish once. Cook on High for 2 to 3 minutes, rotating once.

6. Let stand for 5 minutes before inverting onto serving dish. Some of the topping mixture will remain in the dish. With a spatula spread the mixture on top of the cake and apples. Serve warm.

Cherry-Pecan Bread

YIELD: 1 RING MOLD AND 6 CUPCAKES

2   cups all-purpose flour
½   teaspoon baking soda
½   teaspoon salt
¾   cup sugar
½   cup butter or margarine
2   eggs
1   teaspoon vanilla
¾   cup buttermilk
1   cup chopped pecans
1   (10-ounce) jar maraschino cherries, drained and chopped

Icing:

1   cup confectioners' sugar
¼   teaspoon vanilla
1½ tablespoons milk

1. In mixing bowl, combine flour, soda, and salt; set aside.
2. In large mixer bowl cream sugar and butter. Add eggs and vanilla; mix until light and fluffy. Add flour mixture and buttermilk, mixing just until blended. Fold in pecans and cherries.
3. Remove batter for 6 cupcakes. Each one will bake on High for 1 to 1½ minutes.
4. Pour remaining batter into ring mold. Bake at 60% power for 6 to 7 minutes, rotating dish once. Bake on High for 2 to 3 minutes, rotating dish once.
5. Let stand until cool.
6. Combine icing ingredients and spread over top.

Strawberry-Banana Bread

YIELD: 1 RING MOLD AND 2 CUPCAKES

1½ cups all-purpose flour
⅔ cup sugar
1 teaspoon baking powder
½ teaspoon salt
¾ cup quick-cooking oats
1 cup strawberries
1 banana
⅓ cup vegetable oil
2 eggs, beaten

1. Combine the flour, sugar, baking powder, salt, and oats.
2. Purée the strawberries and banana in a blender or food processor; add to dry ingredients. Blend in oil. Stir in eggs. Continue to stir only until dry ingredients are moistened.
3. Remove enough batter for 2 cupcakes. Bake each cupcake on High for 1 to 1½ minutes. Pour remaining batter into a ring mold and bake on High for 6 to 8 minutes, rotating dish once halfway through.
4. Let stand for 5 minutes to complete cooking. Cool completely.
5. Refrigerate, tightly wrapped, overnight before slicing.

Date-Nut Bread

YIELD: 2 RING MOLDS

1¼ cups water
1 teaspoon baking soda
1 pound dates, chopped
1½ cups sugar
1 cups chopped nuts
2 eggs, beaten
¼ teaspoon salt
2 tablespoons butter or margarine, melted
1 teaspoon vanilla
3½ cups all-purpose flour

1. Bring water and soda to a boil; pour over dates and let cool.
2. Add sugar, nuts, eggs, salt, butter, and vanilla; mix well.
3. Stir in flour.
4. Pour half of batter into ring mold and bake at 60% power for 6 to 7 minutes, rotating dish once. Bake on High for 2 to 3 minutes, rotating dish once.
5. Let stand until cool. Remove from dish and repeat baking instructions with remaining batter.

Lemon Bread

YIELD: 1 RING MOLD

⅓ cup butter
1 cup sugar
2 eggs
1½ cups all-purpose flour
½ cup milk
¾ teaspoon baking powder
1 teaspoon salt
½ cup chopped pecans
    peel of 1 lemon, grated

Glaze:

    juice of 1 lemon
⅓ cup sugar

1. Combine butter, sugar, eggs, flour, milk, baking powder, and salt; mix well with electric mixer. Stir in lemon peel and nuts.
2. Pour batter into ring mold. Bake at 60% power for 6 to 7 minutes, rotating dish once. Bake on High for 2 to 3 minutes, rotating dish once.
3. Let stand for 5 minutes.
4. While still warm, poke small holes (toothpick works well) in top of bread. Combine glaze ingredients and pour over the top.
5. Allow bread to finish cooling and flavors to mellow before slicing.

Sour Cream Nut Bread

YIELD: 1 RING MOLD

1 egg
1 cup dark brown sugar, packed firm
1 cup sour cream
2 tablespoons butter or margarine, melted
2 cups all-purpose flour
¼ teaspoon salt
¼ teaspoon baking powder
½ teaspoon baking soda
½ cup chopped walnuts or pecans

1. Beat egg; add sugar and beat until thick.
2. Add sour cream and butter; beat well.
3. Blend in flour, salt, baking powder, and baking soda.
4. Add nuts.
5. Pour batter into a ring mold. Bake on 60% power for 6 to 7 minutes, rotating dish once. Bake on High for 2 to 3 minutes, rotating dish once.
6. Let stand until cool.

Seafood

Baked Flounder in Lemon Sauce

SERVES 4

1   pound flounder fillets
2   tablespoons butter or margarine, melted
1   tablespoon dried minced onion
1   tablespoon butter or margarine
1   tablespoon flour
¾   cup water
1   chicken bouillon cube
1½ teaspoons parsley, chopped fine
    peel of 1 lemon, grated
1½ tablespoons lemon juice

1. Place flounder in a baking dish and pour melted butter on top. Cover tightly and cook on High for 7 to 8 minutes.

2. Place onion and butter in a small bowl and cook on High for 1 minute. Stir in flour.

3. Dissolve bouillon in water and stir into flour. Cook on High for 1 minute or until slightly thickened. Stir in parsley, lemon peel, and lemon juice. Pour over fish to serve.

Marinated Scallops

SERVES 4

⅓ cup soy sauce
¼ cup wine vinegar
2 tablespoons sugar
½ teaspoon ground ginger
1 garlic clove, pressed
  peel of 1 lime, grated
2 pounds scallops

1. Combine all ingredients except scallops and mix well.
2. Place scallops and marinade in a plastic bag. Refrigerate for at least 1 hour.
3. Pour into a baking dish and spread out in one layer.
4. Cook, covered, on High for 6 to 7 minutes.
5. Serve immediately.

Scallop Rarebit

SERVES 4

1 pound scallops
2 tablespoons butter or margarine
2 tablespoons flour
1 teaspoon salt
  dash of pepper
⅔ cup water
⅓ cup catsup
1 tablespoon prepared mustard
2 cups grated Cheddar cheese
2 eggs, beaten
  toast points

1. Cut the scallops into quarters and place in a baking dish along with butter. Cover and cook on High for 2½ minutes.
2. Blend in flour, salt, and pepper. Gradually add water. Cover and cook on High for 3 minutes or until thickened.
3. Stir in catsup, mustard, and cheese. Cover and cook at 70% power for 1 or 2 minutes.

4. Add eggs carefully to the sauce. Don't let them scramble. Cover and cook at 70% power for 2½ minutes.

5. Serve on toast points.

Hot Crabmeat Sandwich

slice of French bread, toasted
canned crabmeat
tomato slices
fresh mushrooms, sliced
slice of American cheese or Swiss cheese

1. On the French bread layer crabmeat, tomato, mushrooms, and cheese.

2. Place on top of a paper towel on serving dish and place in oven at 70% power just long enough to melt the cheese.

3. Remove paper towel and serve hot.

Hot Seafood Salad

SERVES 4

2 tablespoons butter or margarine
½ green pepper, chopped fine
1 small onion, chopped fine
2 celery stalks, chopped fine
1 cup cooked shrimp (small ones or chopped)
1 (6½-ounce) can crabmeat
1 cup salad dressing or mayonnaise
½ teaspoon salt
dash of hot sauce
buttered bread crumbs

1. In butter, sauté onion, pepper, and celery in covered dish on High for 2 minutes, stirring once.

2. Combine all ingredients except bread crumbs in a cake dish or pie plate. Use a fork to mix all ingredients well. Cover dish and bake at 70% power for 6 minutes or until heated through.

3. Fry bread crumbs in butter in a skillet on the stove. Sprinkle over the top of seafood mixture. Return to oven uncovered for 1 minute on High.

4. Can be served as is or on toasted English muffins.

If there are any leftovers, use as a sandwich. Spread on toasted bread and top with cheese slice, shredded Cheddar cheese, or Swiss cheese. Run under the broiler or in the microwave at 70% power until cheese is melted.

Low-Cal Gumbo

SERVES 8 (about 182 calories per serving)

1 large onion, chopped
3 garlic cloves, minced
1 green pepper, chopped
1 tablespoon chopped parsley
2 (28-ounce) cans whole tomatoes, undrained
1 teaspoon salt
1 teaspoon pepper
2 bay leaves
4 cups okra, cut into pieces
2 (8-ounce) cans tomato sauce
¾ pound frozen crabmeat
¾ pound frozen shrimp
3 cups boiling water

1. Place onion, garlic, green pepper, and ¼ cup liquid from tomatoes into large bowl. Cover tightly with plastic wrap. Cook on High for 2½ minutes, stirring once.

2. Quarter tomatoes and add to bowl along with remaining liquid and parsley. Cover and cook on High for 15 minutes, stirring every 5 minutes.

3. Add salt, pepper, and bay leaves. Cover again and cook for 15 minutes on High, stirring every 5 minutes.

4. Stir in okra and tomato sauce. Cover again and cook on High for 7 minutes, stirring once.

5. Stir in shrimp and crab. Add 3 cups boiling water. Cover and cook for 7 minutes on High, stirring once.

6. Remove bay leaves and serve hot.

Mulled wine (p. 66).

Tuna Casserole

SERVES 4

1 (7½-ounce) package macaroni and cheese dinner
3 tablespoons butter or margarine
1 (16-ounce) can tomatoes, quartered
½ cup milk
1 tablespoon dried minced onion
1 egg, beaten
1 (6½-ounce) can tuna, drained
1 teaspoon seasoned salt

1. Cook macaroni according to package instructions; drain. Add cheese and butter; stir until butter has melted.
2. Stir in tomatoes and half the liquid from the can.
3. Add remaining ingredients. Stir gently to mix ingredients.
4. Bake at 80% power for 4 minutes, stirring after 2 minutes.
5. A crunchy topping is optional.

Tuna-Cashew Casserole

SERVES 4

1 (6½-ounce) can tuna, drained
½ cup coarse-chopped cashews
2 celery stalks, chopped
1 small onion, chopped
1 (10¾-ounce) can cream of mushroom soup
¼ cup dry sherry
1 (5-ounce) can chow mein noddles
  soy sauce

1. In a 1- or 1½-quart bowl, combine the tuna, cashews, celery, onion, soup, and sherry. Cook, uncovered, on High for 4 minutes, stirring once.
2. Serve over chow mein noodles and season with soy sauce.

Top to bottom:
Cream of Tomato Soup (p. 72). Croutons (p. 77).

Macaroni Salad of the Sea

SERVES 6

2   hard-cooked eggs, chopped
1   small onion, chopped
¼   cup chopped celery
¼   cup chopped sweet pickles
¼   cup chopped green pepper
1½ teaspoons chopped pimiento
1   (6½-ounce) can tuna, drained and flaked
¼   cup mayonnaise
1   tablespoon prepared mustard
2   cups cooked elbow macaroni

1. Combine all ingredients except macaroni. Mix well.
2. Gently toss macaroni with other ingredients.
3. Cover and chill overnight.

For an attractive luncheon dish, serve on a platter garnished with ruffled lettuce and tomato slices. Carrot sticks, stuffed celery, and deviled eggs complete the picture.

Lamb

Walnut-glazed Lamb Chops

SERVES 4

4 thick lamb chops
¼ cup honey
1 tablespoon lemon juice
¼ cup chopped walnuts

1. Place chops on roasting rack, cover tightly. Figure cooking time by allowing 14 minutes per pound. Use a 70% power setting.
2. Cook chops for half the time.
3. Combine honey, lemon juice, and walnuts.
4. Remove lamb from the dish and drain grease. Return meat to the dish without the rack. Coat with glaze, cover again, and complete cooking.

Leg of Lamb with Mint

   leg of lamb
   salt, pepper, flour
½ cup chicken broth
¼ cup dry white wine or vermouth
1½ tablespoons dried chopped mint
1 small onion, minced
2 garlic cloves, minced

1. The lamb will cook more evenly if the butcher removes the bone and rolls and ties the roast with string. It will also be much easier to carve. Whether the lamb is rolled or left whole, you should remove the fell (the paperlike covering) from the meat.
2. Rub the lamb with flour seasoned with salt and pepper.

3. Combine remaining ingredients.

4. Place lamb in baking dish and pour sauce over it. Cook at 70% power for about 14 minutes per pound or to 180° on the temperature probe. Baste with juices halfway through.

5. Let stand for 15 minutes before carving.

Greek Marinated Leg of Lamb

SERVES 4 TO 6

3- to 6-pound leg of lamb
½ cup Dijon mustard
2 tablespoons soy sauce
2 tablespoons ground ginger
1 teaspoon thyme
1 garlic clove, pressed
2 tablespoons olive oil

1. The lamb will cook more evenly if the butcher removes the bone and rolls and ties the roast with string. It will also be much easier to carve. Whether the lamb is rolled or left whole, you should remove the fell (the paperlike covering) from the meat.

2. Combine all the marinade ingredients and brush over the lamb.

3. Refrigerate for at least 6 hours.

4. Cook at 70% power for about 14 minutes per pound or to 180° on the temperature probe.

5. Let stand for about 15 minutes before carving.

Beef

Prophet's Stew

SERVES 4

1½ pounds ground beef
1   small onion
3   medium carrots, scraped and chopped
1   large potato, peeled and chopped
¾   cup catsup
    salt and pepper
¾   cup water
1   tablespoon Worcestershire sauce

1. Brown beef and onions on High for 6 minutes, stirring after 3 minutes. Drain grease.
2. In a round bowl combine carrots and potato with 2 tablespoons water. Cover tightly and cook on High for 6 to 8 minutes or until tender. Drain.
3. Combine beef, vegetables, catsup, salt and pepper to taste, water, and Worcestershire sauce. Cover again and cook on 50% power for 5 minutes.

Chili Con Carne

SERVES 2 TO 4

1   pound ground beef
1   envelope onion soup mix
1   tablespoon chili powder
1   (1-pound can) Mexe-Beans or kidney beans
¼   cup water
1   (14½-ounce) can tomatoes, undrained

1. Brown beef on High for 6 minutes, stirring every 2 minutes. Drain grease.

2. Add soup mix, chili powder, beans, water, quartered tomatoes, and tomato liquid. Mix well, cover and cook at 70% power for 10 minutes, stirring every 3 minutes.

3. Let stand for 5 minutes before serving.

Spanish Casserole

SERVES 8

1   small onion, chopped
½   green pepper, chopped
2   tablespoons butter or margarine
1½ pounds ground beef
1   (17-ounce) can corn, drained
1   (10¾-ounce) can tomato soup
1   (4-ounce) can mushroom slices
½   teaspoon salt
1   teaspoon chili powder
1   (5-ounce) package noodles, cooked
½   cup shredded Cheddar cheese

1. Sauté onion and green pepper in butter on High for 2½ minutes.

2. Brown beef on High for 6 to 8 minutes, stirring after every 2 minutes. Drain.

3. In a large bowl, combine beef, onions, peppers, corn, soup, mushrooms, salt, and chili powder.

4. Stir in cooked noodles.

5. Cook at 80% power for 4 minutes, stirring after 2 minutes, or until heated through.

6. Top with shredded cheese and cook at 70% power until cheese is melted.

Taco Salad

SERVES 4

1 pound ground beef
1 small onion, chopped
1 teaspoon chili powder
1 small head lettuce
1 (8-ounce) bottle taco sauce
1 (7-ounce) bag taco-flavored tortilla chips, crushed
  shredded Cheddar cheese

1. Cook beef, onion, and chili powder on High for 6 minutes, stirring once. Drain and set aside.
2. Tear lettuce into bite-size pieces and put in large salad bowl.
3. Add hamburger to lettuce and toss.
4. Add sauce to taste. Start with half the bottle and gradually add more. Mixture should be moist—not soggy.
5. Add tortilla chips and toss so that all ingredients are lightly coated with sauce.
6. Sprinkle shredded Cheddar cheese on top.

Crowd Pleasin' Casserole

SERVES 8

1 pound ground beef
1 onion, chopped
1 (28-ounce) can tomatoes, quartered
1 (10¾-ounce) can cream of mushroom soup
1 tablespoon catsup
1 tablespoon steak sauce
1½ teaspoons dried chopped parsley
1 teaspoon salt
¼ teaspoon pepper
¼ teaspoon sugar
¼ teaspoon ground cinnamon
1 (8-ounce) package elbow macaroni, cooked and drained
1 cup shredded Cheddar cheese

1. Combine ground beef and chopped onion in a plastic colander set in a pie plate. Cook on High for 4 to 6 minutes, stirring once, until browned.

2. In a 3-quart bowl, combine tomatoes and juice from the can with soup, catsup, steak sauce, parsley, salt, pepper, sugar, and cinnamon. Stir to blend.

3. Stir in cooked macaroni.

4. Cover and cook at 50% power for 10 minutes, stirring once.

5. Sprinkle cheese on top and cook at 70% power for 1½ minutes or until cheese melts.

Stuffed Peppers

SERVES 6

1   pound ground beef
1   cup cottage cheese
1   (8-ounce) can tomato sauce
1   egg, beaten
½   cup cracker crumbs
1   tablespoon Worcestershire sauce
1½ teaspoons salt
¼   teaspoon pepper
3   green peppers, cut in half, seeds removed
3   slices American cheese

1. Combine all ingredients except the peppers and American cheese slices. Mix well.

2. Spoon meat mixture into pepper halves. Place in a baking dish and cover. Cook at 70% power for 24 minutes.

3. Top each stuffed pepper with half a piece of cheese. Return to oven at 70% power just long enough to melt cheese.

Stuffed Meat Cups

Meat Cups:

1 pound ground beef
1 egg, beaten
1 slice bread, crumbed
1 tablespoon Kitchen Bouquet sauce
2 tablespoons catsup
½ teaspoon salt
¼ teaspoon pepper

Filling:

1 (4-ounce) can mushroom pieces, drained
1 cup shredded Swiss cheese
¼ cup fine-chopped onion

1. Combine meat cup ingredients; mix well. Set aside one-third of mixture. Divide remaining portion into 4 Pyrex custard cups or 6 muffin cups. Use a spoon to form a shell in each cup.

2. Combine filling ingredients and place an equal portion in each cup.

3. Use remaining meat mixture to shape a top for each cup, sealing the edges.

4. Cook on High for 8 to 10 minutes.

5. Let stand for 5 minutes before serving.

Layered Meatloaf Ring

SERVES 4 TO 6

1½ pounds ground beef
2   eggs, beaten
½   onion, chopped
1   slice bread, crumbed
1   tablespoon Worcestershire sauce
1   teaspoon salt
½   teaspoon pepper
2   cups dry seasoned stuffing mix
¾   cup water
2   tablespoons butter or margarine, melted
1   (4-ounce) can sliced mushrooms, drained
½   onion, sliced

1. Combine ground beef, eggs, chopped onion, bread crumbs, Worcestershire sauce, salt, and pepper; mix well and set aside.

2. Combine stuffing mix (use seasoning packet if there is one), water, and butter.

3. Cover the bottom of a bundt pan or ring mold with mushrooms and onion slices. Top with one-third of the meat mixture. Make the next layer one-half of the stuffing mixture. Repeat layers of meat and stuffing. Finish with layer of meat.

4. Cook, covered, on High for 5 minutes. Reduce power to 50% and cook 8 to 10 minutes.

5. Let stand for 5 minutes.

Monday Night Special

1 pound ground beef
¼ pound ground pork
¼ pound ground veal
½ cup bread crumbs
1 egg, beaten
1 teaspoon prepared mustard
1 teaspoon salt
¼ teaspoon pepper
1 (6-ounce) package sliced mozzarella cheese
¼ cup chopped parsley
½ cup catsup
½ cup water
1 teaspoon horseradish
1 tablespoon Worcestershire sauce

1. Combine meats, bread crumbs, egg, mustard, salt and pepper. Shape into a 12 × 9-inch rectangle. An easy way to do this is to place the meat between two layers of waxed paper and roll flat with a rolling pin. The meat will be of an even thickness with a minimum of mess.

2. Place cheese slices over the meat and sprinkle with parsley. Roll as you would a jelly roll, lifting the waxed paper to help roll. Press ends to seal. Place in a baking dish.

3. Combine catsup, water, horseradish, and Worcestershire; pour sauce over meat. Cook at 70% power for 18 to 20 minutes.

4. Let stand for 5 minutes before serving.

Pizza Hamburger Pie

SERVES 4 TO 6

1   pound ground beef
1½ teaspoons garlic salt or plain salt
¼   teaspoon pepper
1   teaspoon horseradish
1   teaspoon Worcestershire sauce
1   teaspoon prepared mustard
1   (8-ounce) can tomato sauce
2   tablespoons dried minced onion
½   teaspoon oregano
1   cup grated mozzarella cheese

1. Lightly toss beef with salt, pepper, horseradish, Worcestershire sauce, and mustard.

2. Press meat against sides and bottom of an 8- or 9-inch pie plate.

3. Spread tomato sauce over meat and sprinkle with onions, oregano, and cheese.

4. Cook at 70% power for 8 to 10 minutes.

To remove grease from bottom of pie plate, use a basting tube.

Meatloaf with Piquant Sauce

SERVES 6

1   cup bread crumbs
¾   cup milk
2   eggs, beaten
1   tablespoon dried minced onion
1   teaspoon salt
¼   teaspoon pepper
1½ pounds ground beef

Sauce:

½   cup brown sugar
½   cup catsup
2   teaspoons dry mustard
     dash of nutmeg

1. Soak bread crumbs in milk.
2. Stir in eggs, onion, salt, and pepper.
3. Combine all ingredients with ground beef. Shape into a ring mold or a cake dish with an inverted glass in the center.
4. Combine sauce ingredients and blend well. Pour over top of meat mixture.
5. Bake, uncovered, on High for 10 to 12 minutes.
6. Let stand for 5 minutes before serving.

Vegetable Meatloaf

SERVES 6

1½ pounds ground beef
1   (10½-ounce) can vegetable soup, undiluted
½   cup sour cream
¼   cup rolled oats, uncooked
¼   cup dried minced onion
1   (1.5-ounce) package spaghetti sauce mix
1   teaspoon prepared mustard
½   cup catsup

1. Combine all ingredients except catsup; mix well. Place in a ring mold or cake dish with an inverted glass in the center. Bake on High for 5 minutes. Reduce power to 50% and continue baking for 11 minutes.
2. Spread catsup on top.
3. Allow to stand for 5 minutes before serving.

Hash Medley

SERVES 4

1 (15-ounce) can corned beef hash
1 (17-ounce) can corn, drained
1 (16-ounce) can green beans, drained
1 (10¾-ounce) can cream of mushroom soup
½ cup shredded Cheddar cheese
  potato chips or croutons

1. In a 1½-quart bowl, spread hash to form a crust. Be sure sides are high enough to hold the remaining ingredients.
2. Make a layer of corn, green beans, and undiluted soup.
3. Cook, covered, at 80% power for 8 minutes.
4. Sprinkle top of casserole with cheese and crushed potato chips or croutons. Bake, uncovered, at 70% power just long enough to melt cheese.

Beef Stew

SERVES 4

1   pound stew beef, cubed
1   large onion, sliced
1½ teaspoons flour
1   teaspoon salt
¼   teaspoon seasoned pepper
⅛   teaspoon thyme
½   cup catsup
½   cup apple juice or apple cider
2   medium potatoes, peeled and cubed
2   large carrots, scraped and sliced

1. Place meat in 3-quart bowl and sprinkle with flour, stirring to coat. Add remaining ingredients; mix well. Cover tightly and cook on High for 5 minutes; stir. Lower to 50% power and cook for 45 minutes, stirring once or twice.

2. Let stand, covered, for 10 minutes.

Marinated Chuck Roast

SERVES 4

3-pound chuck roast
½ cup strong coffee
½ cup soy sauce
1 tablespoon Worcestershire sauce
1 tablespoon red wine vinegar
8 whole cloves
1 onion, sliced
2 medium potatoes, peeled and cut into eighths
3 medium carrots, scraped and sliced

1. Pierce the meat on both sides with a fork.

2. Combine coffee, soy sauce, Worcestershire, vinegar, and cloves in a large bowl or plastic bag. Place meat in marinade and let stand at room temperature for several hours or refrigerate overnight. Turn meat occasionally.

3. Place meat and marinade in a very large bowl so the meat can lie flat and there will be room for vegetables to be added. Cover tightly and cook on High for 12 minutes.

4. Turn roast over and add vegetables. Cover again and cook at 50% power for 1 hour. Use a basting tube to make sure vegetables are coated with marinade every 15 minutes.

5. Let stand for 10 to 15 minutes before serving.

One More Time!

SERVES 4

1 or 2 large onions, sliced and separated
1 teaspoon sugar
1 tablespoon butter or margarine
3 cups mashed potatoes, seasoned
6 slices cooked roast beef
1 (17-ounce) can peas, drained
1 (10¼-ounce) can beef gravy or 1 cup leftover gravy
2 tablespoons grated Parmesan cheese
  paprika

1. Put onions in a hot, dry skillet and sprinkle with sugar. Cook on stove, stirring constantly until lightly browned. Add butter and continue cooking until tender. Remove from heat.

2. Spread half the mashed potatoes in a baking dish and arrange meat on top. Spread onions over the meat and then the peas and gravy. Cover with remaining mashed potatoes.

3. Cook, covered, on 80% power for 6 to 8 minutes.

Beef Strips with Dumplings

SERVES 4 TO 6

1½ pounds round steak
¼ cup flour
  salt and pepper
2 celery stalks, chopped
1 (16-ounce) can whole tomatoes, undrained
1 envelope dry onion soup mix

DUMPLINGS:

1 cup biscuit mix
⅓ cup milk
1 tablespoon chopped chives

TOPPING:

½ **to 1 cup shredded Cheddar cheese**

1. Cut beef into ¼-inch strips.
2. Place flour in a 3-quart casserole and season with salt and pepper. Add beef strips and toss to coat with flour.
3. Add celery, quartered tomatoes, and onion soup mixed with liquid from the tomatoes. Cover tightly and cook on High for 5 minutes. Stir.
4. Cover again and cook at 50% power for 20 to 25 minutes, stirring after 10 minutes.
5. Combine dumpling ingredients. Drop by spoonfuls on top of meat mixture. Cook, uncovered, at 50% power for 8 minutes or until firm. They will still be white.
6. Sprinkle top of dumplings with cheese. Cook, uncovered, at 70% power for 1½ minutes or until cheese melts.

Swiss Steak

SERVES 4

1½ **pounds round steak**
   flour seasoned with salt and pepper
1 **medium onion, chopped**
¼ **cup chopped celery**
1 **(8-ounce) can tomato sauce**
1 **(14½-ounce) can whole tomatoes, quartered**

1. Trim fat from meat and cut into 4 serving-size pieces. Dredge through flour. Pound with meat mallet or edge of saucer.
2. Place in a 2-quart baking dish. Top with onion, celery, tomato sauce mixed with half the liquid from tomato can, and tomatoes. Cover tightly and cook on High for 6 to 8 minutes.
3. Reduce power to 60% and cook for 30 to 40 minutes, rotating dish once.
4. Let stand, covered, for 5 minutes before serving.

Swiss Steak Supreme

SERVES 4

1½ pounds round steak
¼ cup flour
1½ teaspoons dry English-style mustard
   salt
   fresh ground pepper
   oil
1   onion sliced and separated into rings
1   carrot, scraped and sliced thin
1   (16-ounce) can tomatoes, quartered; reserve juice
1   tablespoon brown sugar
2   tablespoons Worcestershire sauce
¼   teaspoon dried parsley

1. Cut steak into 4 serving-size portions.
2. In a small bowl, combine flour and mustard.
3. Dredge each piece of meat in the flour, sprinkle with salt and pepper, and pound with a meat mallet or the edge of a saucer. Coat again with any remaining flour.
4. Heat a small amount of oil in a skillet on the stove. Brown the meat.
5. Place the meat in a flat baking dish so that no pieces overlap. Top with onion slices, carrots, and tomatoes.
6. Stir the sugar, Worcestershire sauce, and parsley into the tomato juice reserved from the can. Pour over the top of the meat.
7. Cover dish tightly with plastic wrap. Cook for 6 minutes on High. Rotate dish and cook for 30 to 40 minutes at 60% power.
8. Let stand for 5 minutes before serving.

Beef Stroganoff

SERVES 4

1½ pounds sirloin steak, cut into strips
    oil
1   tablespoon butter or margarine
1   onion, sliced
1   garlic clove, minced
1   cup sliced mushrooms
1   (10½-ounce) can beef broth
¼   cup dry red wine
2   tablespoons cornstarch
1   cup sour cream
    cooked noodles

1. Using a small amount of oil in a frying pan, brown the beef strips on the stove. Set the beef aside.

2. Sauté the onions and garlic in butter on High for 1 to 2 minutes or until tender. Remove from dish and sauté mushrooms at 70% power for 1½ to 2 minutes.

3. Stir cornstarch into wine until all lumps are gone.

4. Combine all ingredients except sour cream and noodles. Cook, covered, at 70% power for 18 to 20 minutes or until meat is tender.

5. Stir in sour cream and continue cooking at 70% power for 3 minutes or until heated through.

6. Serve over hot noodles.

Pork

Apple and Raisin Pork Chops

SERVES 4

4 pork chops
  oil
  salt and pepper to taste
2 cooking apples, pared, cored, and sliced into rings
¼ cup brown sugar
2 tablespoons flour
1 cup hot water
1 tablespoon tarragon vinegar
½ cup raisins

1. Brown the chops in a skillet on the stove using a small amount of oil. Place in a baking dish and sprinkle with salt and pepper to taste. Top with apple rings and brown sugar.

2. Add flour to the drippings in the skillet and stir until lightly browned. Add water and vinegar and cook, stirring, until thick. Add raisins. Pour over chops.

3. Cover tightly and bake at 70% power, allowing 5 minutes per pound.

Chili Chops

SERVES 6

6 pork chops, about 1½ pounds total
1 teaspoon seasoned salt
4 tablespoons flour
   oil
2½ cups water
1 (8-ounce) can tomato sauce
3 tablespoons dried minced onion
1½ teaspoons salt
1 (1¼-ounce) envelope chili seasoning mix
2 cups cooked rice

1. Dredge pork chops in flour and seasoned salt. In skillet with small amount of oil, brown chops.

2. In a baking dish, combine water, tomato sauce, onion, salt, and chili seasoning. Bring to a boil on High, about 6 to 8 minutes, stirring once.

3. Stir cooked rice into sauce. Place pork chops on rice and cook, covered, at 70% power for 12 to 14 minutes.

4. Let stand covered, for 5 minutes before serving.

Honey-Curry Pork Chops

SERVES 6

Make the sauce for this dish the day before you plan to serve it.

4 slices bacon, diced
1 small onion, chopped
2 garlic cloves, minced
½ cup teriyaki sauce or soy sauce
⅓ cup lemon juice
2 tablespoons honey
1½ teaspoons curry powder
1 teaspoon chili powder
½ teaspoon salt
6 pork chops

1. Cook diced bacon on High for 4 minutes or until crisp. Remove bacon from grease and set aside.

2. In the bacon grease, sauté the onion and garlic on High for 2 minutes, stirring once. Drain the grease.

3. In a 4-cup measure, combine all ingredients except pork chops. Cook at 50% power for 2 minutes, stirring once. Let stand for 2 hours for flavors to blend.

4. Arrange chops in a baking dish. Pour sauce over top, cover tightly with plastic wrap, and refrigerate overnight.

5. Allow chops to come to room temperature.

6. Bake, covered, at 70% power for 5 to 7 minutes per pound. To check for doneness, use tip of knife in meat near the bone to see if the meat is gray rather than pink.

7. Let stand, covered, for 5 minutes before serving.

Creamy Mushroom Stuffed Chops

SERVES 4

4 (6-ounce) pork loin chops
   salt and pepper
1 (2½-ounce) jar sliced mushrooms, drained
½ cup grated Swiss cheese
2 tablespoons parsley flakes
½ teaspoon sage
1 (10¾-ounce) can cream of mushroom soup
¼ cup white wine

1. Cut pockets in the chops and season with salt and pepper.

2. Place on a roasting rack in a baking dish, cover, and cook at 70% power for 8 minutes.

3. Remove rack and drain grease.

4. Combine mushrooms, cheese, parsley, and sage. Stuff the chops.

5. Combine soup and wine and pour over the chops. Cook, covered, at 70% power for 10 to 11 minutes, spooning sauce over the chops once.

6. Let stand, covered, for 5 minutes before serving.

Pork Chops with Tomatoes

SERVES 4

4 pork chops, about 1 pound
  flour
  salt and pepper
  oil
1 small onion, chopped
½ green pepper, chopped
1 (28-ounce) can tomatoes
1 tablespoon Worcestershire sauce
1 tablespoon lemon juice
1 tablespoon sugar
1 beef bouillon cube

1. Dredge the pork chops in flour seasoned with salt and pepper.

2. Lightly brown chops in a skillet with a small amount of oil. Place in a baking dish.

3. Sauté onion and green pepper in the skillet.

4. Quarter the tomatoes over the skillet so the juice goes in with the onion and peppers. Add tomatoes.

5. In a 2-cup measure or a bowl, combine the juice from the can of tomatoes, Worcestershire sauce, lemon juice, sugar, and bouillon cube. Cook on High for 2 minutes. Add to the ingredients in the skillet and stir.

6. Pour tomato sauce over the pork chops. Cover tightly and bake at 70% power for 4 to 6 minutes.

7. Let stand, covered, for 5 minutes before serving.

Pork Chops in Creole Rice

SERVES 4

4 pork chops
  oil
1 onion, sliced and separated into rings
2 celery stalks, chopped
1 green pepper, cut into strips
1 garlic clove, diced
2 (8-ounce) cans tomato sauce
1 cup hot water
2 tablespoons brown sugar
1 teaspoon salt
1 teaspoon dried parsley flakes
1 cup quick-cooking rice

1. Pour a small amount of oil into a skillet and, on the stove, brown the pork chops. Remove from the skillet.

2. Sauté onion, celery, green pepper, and garlic in the drippings.

3. In a bowl, combine tomato sauce, water, brown sugar, salt, parsley, and rice. Add sautéed vegetables and drippings.

4. Pour into a glass baking dish large enough to hold the pork chops so they will not overlap each other. Do not add pork chops yet. Cover tightly with plastic wrap and cook on High for 5 minutes, stirring once.

5. Place pork chops on top of rice mixture. Cover again and bake at 70% power for about 8 minutes.

6. Let stand, covered, for 5 to 10 minutes before serving.

Barbecued Spareribs

SERVES 4

3   pounds pork spareribs cut into serving pieces
1   small onion, quartered
½   green pepper, quartered
2   garlic cloves
1   teaspoon Worcestershire sauce
1½ teaspoons barbecue seasoning
¾   cup catsup
½   cup dark brown sugar
¼   cup dark molasses
¼   cup lemon juice
1   teaspoon dry mustard

1. Set the spareribs aside. Combine remaining ingredients in a blender or food processor until smooth.

2. Place half the ribs in a large baking dish and cover tightly. Cook at 70% power for 8 minutes, drain. Repeat with remaining spareribs.

3. At this point, ribs may be placed on a grill and basted. If they are to be finished in the microwave, baste half the ribs with sauce, cover, and cook at 70% power for about 15 minutes. Repeat with the remaining ribs.

Ham Rolls Continental

SERVES 4

8 thin slices boiled ham
8 slices Swiss cheese
1 (10-ounce) package frozen broccoli or asparagus, cooked
   and drained
1 onion, sliced and separated into rings
2 tablespoons butter or margarine
2 tablespoons flour
½ teaspoon salt
¼ teaspoon basil
   dash of pepper
1 cup milk

1. Top each ham slice with a slice of cheese.
2. Add two or three spears of broccoli or asparagus on top of the cheese.
3. Roll up and secure with a toothpick if necessary. Place in a baking dish, leaving a small amount of space between each one.
4. In a skillet on the stove, brown the onion slices in butter until they are a light golden color.
5. Stir the flour, salt, basil, and pepper into the onions.
6. Gradually add the milk and stir until thickened. Spoon sauce over the top of the ham rolls.
7. Cover the dish and heat at 70% power for 5 minutes.

Saucy Ham

SERVES 4

1   center-cut cooked ham steak (1½ pounds, 1-inch thick)
½ cup ginger ale
½ cup orange juice
     peel of 1 orange, grated
¼ cup brown sugar, packed firm
1½ tablespoons vegetable oil
1½ teaspoons wine vinegar
1   teaspoon dry mustard
½ teaspoon ground allspice
¼ teaspoon ground cloves

1. Combine all ingredients, except ham, and blend.
2. Place ham in a baking dish and cover with half the sauce. Marinate for 1 hour at room temperature.
3. Cover and cook at 70% power for 15 minutes.
4. Warm remaining sauce on High for 1½ minutes. Serve with the ham.

Ham with Raisin Sauce

SERVES 4

1 center-cut cooked ham steak (1½ pounds, 1-inch thick)
½ cup raisins
½ cup hot water
½ cup red currant jelly
   peel of 1 orange, grated
½ cup orange juice
2 tablespoons brown sugar
1 tablespoon cornstarch
   dash salt
2 dashes ground allspice
1 teaspoon Dijon mustard

1. Combine raisins, water, jelly, orange peel, and orange juice in a 4-cup glass measure. Cook on High for 2½ to 3½ minutes, stirring once, or until boiling.
2. Combine brown sugar, cornstarch, salt, allspice, and mustard. Stir into orange mixture. Cook on High for 1 to 1½ minutes, stirring once or twice. Mixture should be slightly thickened and clear.
3. In a baking dish cook ham slice at 70% power, covered, for 5 to 8 minutes or until heated through.
4. Pour sauce over ham to serve.

Ham Loaf

SERVES 6

1 (8¼-ounce) can crushed pineapple
2 tablespoons brown sugar
1 cup rolled oats
¼ cup tomato juice
1 to 1½ pounds ground cooked ham
½ pound bulk sausage
½ green pepper, chopped
2 eggs, beaten
¼ teaspoon salt

1. Drain the pineapple and reserve ¼ cup liquid. Stir brown sugar into the juice.
2. Pour juice mixture into oats; stir.
3. Add all remaining ingredients. Mix well—use your hands.
4. Place in a ring mold. Bake at 70% power for 25 to 30 minutes.
5. Let stand for 5 minutes before serving.

Plantation Casserole

SERVES 6

2 cups chopped cooked ham
1 cup cooked peas, drained
1 (17-ounce) can creamed corn
¼ pound American cheese, cubed
¼ cup chopped onion
1 cup evaporated milk
1 tablespoon Worcestershire sauce
1 cup biscuit mix
½ cup cornmeal
2 tablespoons sugar
½ teaspoon salt
1 egg, beaten

1. Combine ham, peas, corn, cheese, onion, ½ cup milk, and Worcestershire sauce. Pour into a greased casserole and bake at 400°for 10 minutes.

2. Combine biscuit mix, cornmeal, sugar, salt, egg, and ½ cup milk and blend just until all ingredients are moistened. Pour around edge of meat mixture. Bake 20 minutes longer.

Cook ham and peas in the microwave for this dish. The rest of the preparation is done in the conventional oven since the bread portion would not crust if done in the microwave.

Cheesy Ham and Eggs

SERVES 4 TO 6

¼ cup butter or margarine
¼ cup flour
2 cups milk
1½ teaspoons prepared mustard
2 teaspoons Worcestershire sauce
1 cup shredded Cheddar cheese
1 cup diced cooked ham
6 hard-cooked eggs, peeled and halved
4 to 6 slices bread, toasted

1. Melt butter in a 1½-quart bowl. Stir in flour.
2. Pour milk into a 4-cup measure and heat on High for 1 minute.
3. Stir milk into flour and cook at 70% power for 6 to 7 minutes, stirring after 4 minutes. Mixture should thicken.
4. Add mustard, Worcestershire, and cheese. Cook at 70% power for 30 seconds or until cheese is melted.
5. Stir in ham.
6. Fold in eggs. Cook at 70% power for 1 to 2 minutes.
7. Serve on toast.

Macaroni and Ham Salad

SERVES 8

4 cups cooked elbow macaroni
3 hard-cooked eggs, chopped
1 cup chopped cooked ham
2 tablespoons chopped pimiento
½ cup sliced green olives
⅔ cup sour cream
⅓ cup salad dressing or mayonnaise
1 teaspoon salt
½ teaspoon dry mustard

1. Combine macaroni, eggs, ham, pimiento, and olives.
2. Combine sour cream, salad dressing, salt, and mustard; mix well.
3. Pour sauce over macaroni mixture and toss gently.
4. Chill.

Canadian Bacon Casserole

SERVES 4

1 (7¼-ounce) package macaroni and cheese dinner
½ green pepper, diced
½ medium onion, chopped
1 tablespoon butter or margarine
1 (10¾-ounce) can cream of celery soup
6 to 8 slices Canadian bacon

1. Prepare macaroni dinner according to package directions.
2. Sauté pepper and onion in butter on High for 2 minutes.
3. Combine macaroni, pepper, onion, and undiluted celery soup in a bowl. Top with slices of Canadian bacon. Cook at 70% power for 7 minutes or until heated through.

Poultry

Honey-glazed Chicken

SERVES 4

2½ to 3-pound chicken
¼ cup honey
1 tablespoon teriyaki sauce
1 teaspoon rum
1 teaspoon dark molasses
1½ teaspoons Dijon mustard
1½ teaspoons catsup

1. Prepare chicken for cooking by tying legs and wings close to body and shielding thin areas with foil.
2. Combine all glaze ingredients and blend well. Baste chicken with glaze.
3. Cook, uncovered, on High for 7 to 8 minutes per pound.
4. Let stand 10 minutes before carving.
5. Drizzle remaining glaze over carved slices of chicken.

Lemony Chicken

SERVES 4 TO 6

1 chicken, cut up and with skin removed
1 lemon
  flour
  seasoned salt
  oil
  brown sugar
2 chicken bouillon cubes
  chopped mint

1. Grate lemon peel and set aside.
2. Using half the lemon, squeeze juice over chicken parts and rub in well.
3. Shake chicken in bag of flour and seasoned salt to taste.
4. Brown pieces in skillet with a small amount of oil.
5. Transfer pieces to a baking dish. Sprinkle each piece with brown sugar. Slice thin the remaining lemon half and top each piece of chicken with a slice.
6. Dissolve the bouillon cubes in 1 cup of hot water. Pour broth into dish, not over the top of the chicken. Sprinkle the chicken with chopped mint and lemon peel.
7. Bake, uncovered, on High for about 5 minutes per pound.
8. Let stand for 5 minutes before serving.

Marinated Chuck Roast (p. 101).

Sweet Lemon Chicken

SERVES 4 TO 6

1 whole chicken, cut up
  flour
  salt
  oil
1 (6-ounce) can frozen lemonade concentrate, thawed and
    undiluted
¼ cup water
3 tablespoons brown sugar
3 tablespoons catsup
1 tablespoon vinegar
1 tablespoon cornstarch
1 tablespoon cold water
2 cups cooked rice

1. Season flour with salt. Dredge chicken in mixture.

2. Brown pieces in a small amount of oil in a skillet. Drain chicken on paper toweling and set aside.

3. In a 4-cup measure, combine lemonade concentrate, water, brown sugar, catsup, and vinegar; stir well. Bring to a boil on High, stirring once.

4. Place chicken in a baking dish and pour sauce over pieces. Cover tightly and bake on High for 6 to 8 minutes.

5. Combine pan drippings and enough water to make 1½ cups liquid.

6. Combine cornstarch and cold water, stirring until smooth. Add to pan drippings and water. Cook on High for 2½ minutes, stirring once, until smooth and thick.

7. Serve sauce over hot rice.

Sweet and Sour Chicken (p. 126).

Banana-Orange Chicken

SERVES 4

4 chicken breast halves, skinned and boned
1⅓ cups bread cubes
⅓ cup chopped pecans
3 tablespoons butter, melted
1 banana, mashed
¼ cup frozen orange juice concentrate
¼ cup dark corn syrup
1 tablespoon lemon juice

1. Combine bread cubes, pecans, and butter.
2. Lightly pound the chicken breasts. Place one-fourth of bread mixture in center of each breast. Fold chicken over and secure with toothpick.
3. Arrange chicken pieces in a baking dish.
4. Combine banana, orange juice, corn syrup, and lemon juice. Spoon over each piece of chicken. Cover tightly and cook on High for 15 minutes.
5. Let stand for 5 minutes before serving.

Cherry Chicken

SERVES 4

4 chicken breast halves, skinned
2 to 3 tablespoons oil
1 (21-ounce) can cherry pie filling
½ cup dry white wine
½ cup orange juice
1 tablespoon grated orange peel
¼ cup dark brown sugar
½ teaspoon salt
¼ teaspoon ground allspice
¼ teaspoon ground cloves
  slivered almonds

1. Lightly brown chicken in oil in a skillet.
2. Arrange chicken in a casserole and cook, covered, on High for 8 minutes. Drain grease.
3. Combine remaining ingredients and pour over chicken. Cook, covered, on 50% power for 3 to 4 minutes.
4. Let stand for 5 minutes. Serve with rice.

Chicken Cacciatore

SERVES 4

4 chicken breast halves, skinned
1 large onion, sliced and separated into rings
½ cup dry white wine
1 (14½-ounce) can whole tomatoes, drained
1 (8-ounce) can tomato sauce
1 garlic clove, pressed
1 teaspoon oregano
½ teaspoon salt
¼ teaspoon thyme

1. Arrange chicken in a baking dish. Place onion rings on top.
2. Combine remaining ingredients; pour over top of chicken.
3. Cover tightly and cook on High for 20 minutes.
4. Let stand for 5 minutes. Serve with rice.

Chicken and Rice Casserole

SERVES 4

4 chicken breast halves, skinned and boned
1 (10¾-ounce) can cream of chicken soup
¾ soup can of water
½ to 1 package dry onion soup mix
⅔ cup quick-cooking rice
1 tablespoon butter or margarine, melted
3 tablespoons soy sauce

1. Combine chicken soup, water, onion soup mix, and rice. Pour into a 2-quart baking dish.

2. Combine soy sauce with melted butter. Dip each piece of chicken in the sauce. Lay chicken on top of rice. Cover dish tightly and cook on High for 6 minutes and at 60% power for 15 minutes.

3. Let stand for 5 minutes before serving.

Islander Chicken

SERVES 4

4 chicken breast halves, boned and skinned
1 (20-ounce) can pineapple chunks, drained, ½ to ¾ cup
    liquid reserved
½ cup butter or margarine, melted
1 envelope dry onion soup mix
1 tablespoon cornstarch
2 tablespoons fresh lime juice
    peel of 1 lime, grated

1. Arrange chicken and pineapple chunks in a baking dish.

2. Combine butter, soup mix, cornstarch, ½ cup pineapple juice, lime juice, and lime peel and mix well. Pour sauce over the chicken and pineapple chunks.

3. Cook, covered, on High for 14 to 16 minutes.

4. Let stand for 5 minutes before serving.

Chicken Parmesan

SERVES 4

4 chicken breast halves, skinned and boned
2 eggs, beaten
1 teaspoon salt
   dash of pepper
1 cup dry bread crumbs
½ cup oil
2 (8-ounce) cans tomato sauce
1 teaspoon sugar
1 teaspoon oregano
1 garlic clove, pressed
1 tablespoon butter or margarine
   grated Parmesan cheese
8 ounces sliced mozzarella cheese

1. Pound chicken breasts with a meat mallet or edge of a saucer.

2. Combine eggs, salt, and pepper. Dip chicken in egg batter and roll in bread crumbs.

3. In a skillet, heat the oil. Brown each side of the chicken quickly. Remove from skillet and place in a baking dish.

4. Pour remaining oil out of skillet and combine tomato sauce, sugar, oregano, and garlic. Bring to a boil, reduce heat, and simmer for 10 minutes. Stir in butter until melted. Pour sauce over chicken.

5. Sprinkle top with Parmesan cheese.

6. Cover tightly and cook on High for 5 minutes.

7. Place slices of mozzarella to cover top. Leave uncovered and return to oven at 70% power for 1½ minutes to melt cheese.

Chicken Rolls with Beef

SERVES 4

4 chicken breast halves, skinned and boned
2 slices bacon
1 (2½-ounce) jar sliced dried beef
1 (10¾-ounce) can golden mushroom soup
½ cup sour cream

1. Roll up each piece of chicken and wrap with ½ piece of bacon.
2. Spread beef on the bottom of a baking dish and placed rolled chicken breasts on top.
3. Combine mushroom soup and sour cream. Pour over chicken.
4. Cover dish tightly and bake on High for 12 to 14 minutes.
5. Let stand for 5 minutes before serving.

Chicken Enchiladas

SERVES 4

8 canned or frozen corn tortillas

Filling:
2 cups chopped cooked chicken
1 cup cottage cheese
½ cup chopped olives
2 teaspoons parsley flakes
½ teaspoon salt
⅛ teaspoon pepper
⅛ teaspoon garlic powder

Sauce:
1 small onion, chopped
½ green pepper, chopped
1 (15-ounce) can tomato sauce
1 (4-ounce) can green chilies, drained and chopped
2 teaspoons chili powder
1 teaspoon sugar
⅛ teaspoon garlic powder

Topping:

1½ cups shredded Cheddar cheese

1. Combine filling ingredients in mixing bowl. Spoon equal portions down center of each tortilla and roll up. Place in a baking dish.

2. Combine onion and pepper in a bowl, cover, and cook on High for 3 to 4 minutes. Stir in remaining sauce ingredients; pour over tortillas. Cover and cook at 70% power for 8 to 9 minutes.

3. Sprinkle with cheese and cook on 70% power for 1½ minutes or until cheese is melted.

Casserole Olé

SERVES 6

8   taco shells or tortillas, broken in pieces
1   (10¾-ounce) can cream of mushroom soup
1   (10¾-ounce) can cream of chicken soup
1   (5.3-ounce) can evaporated milk
1   (5-ounce) can chunk chicken or 1 cup chopped cooked
        chicken
1   (4-ounce) can chopped green chilies, drained
1   teaspoon chili powder
1½ cups shredded Cheddar cheese

1. Arrange broken taco shells in the bottom of a baking dish.

2. In a bowl, combine all the remaining ingredients except the cheese. Cook on High for 4 minutes, stirring twice. Pour over shells and top with cheese.

3. Bake, covered, at 50% power for 4½ minutes.

Sweet and Sour Chicken

SERVES 4 TO 6

¼ cup dark brown sugar, packed firm
½ teaspoon salt
¾ cup liquid from canned pineapple
¼ cup vinegar
1 tablespoon soy sauce
1 medium onion, sliced
1 green pepper, sliced into rings
½ cup thin celery strips
2 tablespoons cornstarch
3 cups cooked chicken, sliced into strips
1 (20-ounce) can pineapple chunks, drained; reserve liquid
2 tablespoons chopped pimiento
¼ cup slivered almonds
1 (5-ounce) can chow mein noodles

1. In a large bowl, combine brown sugar, salt, pineapple liquid, vinegar, soy sauce, onion, pepper rings, and celery. Cook, covered, on High for 5 minutes, stirring once.
2. Stir in cornstarch until all lumps are gone. Cook, covered, on High for 2 minutes or until mixture begins to thicken.
3. Stir in chicken, pineapple chunks, and pimiento. Cook, covered, on High for 2 minutes or until warm.
4. Sprinkle top with almonds.
5. Serve over chow mein noodles.

Springtime Chicken on Dressing

SERVES 6

1 (8-ounce) package herb-seasoned stuffing mix
3 tablespoons butter
3 tablespoons flour
1 cup chicken broth
½ cup cream
2 cups diced cooked chicken
1 (17-ounce) can small peas, drained
2 cups shredded carrots
1 small onion, chopped
  salt and pepper to taste

1. Mix stuffing according to package directions. Spread in the bottom of a 2½-quart baking dish.

2. In a large bowl, melt the butter.

3. Stir in flour until smooth. Cook on High for 45 seconds. Stir well.

4. Stir in broth. Cook on High for 2 minutes or until boiling. Stir well.

5. Stir in cream. Add chicken, peas, carrots, and onion. Season to taste.

6. Spread chicken and vegetables on top of stuffing. At this point, final cooking may be done in the microwave or in a conventional oven. The stuffing will be very moist if done in the microwave or crisp if done conventionally. In the microwave, bake at 70% power for 8 to 10 minutes or until heated through. In a conventional oven, bake at 400° for 15 minutes.

Creamed Chicken and Ham

SERVES 6

¼ cup butter or margarine
¼ cup chopped onion
¼ cup flour
1 tablespoon prepared mustard
½ teaspoon salt
¼ teaspoon cayenne pepper
1 (13-ounce) can evaporated milk
1 (4-ounce) can mushrooms, drained
1 cup cubed cooked chicken
1½ cups cubed cooked ham
¼ cup sliced olives

1. Place butter and onion in a bowl and cover tightly. Cook on High for 1 to 2 minutes.

2. Stir in flour, mustard, salt, and cayenne pepper.

3. Gradually add milk. Blend until smooth. Cook on High for 2 minutes, stirring after 1 minute.

4. Stir in remaining ingredients. Cook at 50% power for 4 minutes, stirring after 2 minutes.

5. Serve over toast points, toasted buns, or toasted English muffins.

Tantalizing Chicken Tetrazzini

SERVES 4 TO 6

8 ounces spaghetti, broken in half
1 tablespoon butter or margarine
2 tablespoons butter or margarine
¼ cup flour
1 teaspoon salt
½ teaspoon celery salt
½ teaspoon paprika
⅛ teaspoon pepper
1½ cups milk
2 chicken bouillon cubes
¾ cup Parmesan cheese
3 cups chopped cooked chicken
1 (4-ounce) jar mushroom pieces, drained
¼ cup pimiento strips

1. Cook the spaghetti according to package directions; drain. Stir in 1 tablespoon butter until melted. Set aside.

2. In a large bowl, melt 2 tablespoons butter. Stir in flour, salt, celery salt, paprika, and pepper; blend well. Gradually add milk. Dissolve bouillon cubes in 1 cup boiling water. Stir into sauce. Cook on High for 6 to 8 minutes, uncovered, stirring every 2 minutes. Sauce should be thickened.

3. Stir ½ cup of cheese into sauce.

4. Add spaghetti, chicken, mushrooms, and pimiento to sauce. Use two forks to blend all ingredients.

5. Sprinkle remaining ¼ cup cheese on top of casserole. Bake at 70% power for 4 to 8 minutes or until heated through.

Chicken Strata

SERVES 4 TO 6

1 small onion, chopped
2 or 3 celery stalks, chopped
½ green pepper, chopped
3 cups cubed cooked chicken (or turkey)
½ cup mayonnaise
1½ teaspoons salt
   dash of pepper
6 slices day-old bread, cubed
2 eggs, beaten
1⅓ cups milk
1 (10¾-ounce) can cream of mushroom soup
¾ cup shredded Cheddar cheese

1. Combine onion, celery, and green pepper in a small bowl and cook on High for 3 to 4 minutes, stirring once.

2. Combine chicken, mayonnaise, salt, and pepper. Stir in sautéed vegetables.

3. Place half the bread cubes in the bottom of a round baking dish. Top with half the chicken mixture. Repeat the layers.

4. Combine the eggs and milk; pour over the casserole. Refrigerate overnight or for at least 1 hour.

5. Top casserole with the mushroom soup. Bake at 70% power for 12 minutes.

6. Sprinkle cheese on top and continue baking at 70% power for 3 minutes.

Mama's Best Chicken Casserole

SERVES 6

2½   pound chicken, cooked, removed from bones, and chopped
2   cups cooked rice
2   celery stalks, chopped
1   small onion, chopped
½   cup slivered almonds or chopped pecans
¾   cup salad dressing or mayonnaise
¼   cup water
1   (10¾-ounce) can cream of chicken soup
1   (4-ounce) can mushroom pieces, drained
1   tablespoon lemon juice
1   teaspoon salt
¼   teaspoon pepper
2   hard-cooked eggs, sliced

1. Combine all ingredients, except eggs, and mix well.
2. Add egg slices and gently toss.
3. Cook at 50% power for 8 minutes or until heated through.

Chicken Stew

SERVES 8

1   tablespoon butter or margarine
¼   cup chopped celery
1   small onion, sliced
4   cups cooked chicken, cut into bite-size pieces
1   potato, cooked and diced
1   (17-ounce) can cream-style corn
3½   cups tomato juice
1½   teaspoons salt
4   tablespoons prepared mustard
1   tablespoon Worcestershire sauce
¼   teaspoon cayenne pepper

1. Sauté onion and celery in butter.
2. Combine all ingredients in a large bowl and cook, covered, on 80% power for about 15 minutes, stirring every 5 minutes.

Chicken and Fruit Salad

SERVES 6

2   to 3 cups chopped, chicken cooked
1   tablespoon salad oil
1   tablespoon orange juice
1   tablespoon vinegar
½   teaspoon salt
1½ cups cooked rice
1   cup seedless grapes
¾   cups sliced, celery
1   cup canned pineapple chunks, halved
1   (11-ounce) can mandarin orange sections, drained
½   cup toasted slivered almonds
¼   cup mayonnaise
    fresh parsley

1. Combine chicken, oil, orange juice, vinegar, and salt in a large bowl and set aside for 30 minutes to allow flavors to blend.
2. Add remaining ingredients and toss gently.
3. Garnish top with orange sections and parsley.

Lime and Melon Chicken Salad

SERVES 6

3   cups diced, cooked chicken
2   cups cooked rice, chilled
2   green onions, sliced
1   cantaloupe, scooped into balls or chopped

Dressing:

¾ cup salad dressing or mayonnaise
   peel of 1 lime, grated
3 tablespoons lime juice
1 teaspoon curry powder
1 teaspoon salt
   white pepper to taste
   toasted sliced almonds for garnish

1. Combine chicken, rice, onions, and cantaloupe.
2. Stir together dressing ingredients.
3. Toss chicken mixture with dressing.
4. Sprinkle almonds on top.
5. Serve chilled.

Fruit Stuffing

YIELD: FOR 10-TO 12-POUND TURKEY

1 cup chopped pitted prunes
1 cup cranberries, rinsed and drained
1 cup chopped dried apricots
1 (8-ounce) package herb-seasoned stuffing mix
4 tablespoons sugar
1 cup chicken broth

1. Gently toss all ingredients together.
2. Do not salt cavity of turkey.
3. When filling the cavity, leave some room for expansion.
4. Stuffing does not increase the cooking time.

Tempting Turkey Casserole

SERVES 6

12 slices bread
2 cups turkey cooked, diced
1 cup chopped celery
1 small onion, chopped
1 (4½-ounce) jar mushrooms, drained
4 eggs, beaten
1 cup mayonnaise
2 cups milk
1 (10¾-ounce) can cream of mushroom soup
¼ cup grated cheese

1. Butter bread on both sides; trim crust. Lay six slices on bottom of a 2-quart baking dish.

2. Combine turkey, celery, onion, and mushrooms and spread over bread. Top with remaining slices of bread.

3. Mix eggs and mayonnaise until smooth; stir in milk and pour over bread.

4. Cover and refrigerate overnight.

5. Spread mushroom soup over top. Cook, covered, on High for 20 minutes. During last 2 or 3 minutes, remove cover, sprinkle with cheese, and reduce power to 70%.

6. Let stand for 5 minutes before serving.

Turkey Thermidor

SERVES 6 TO 8

2 cups diced cooked turkey
1 (10-ounce) package frozen peas, cooked and drained
1 cup chopped celery
1 (5-ounce) can water chestnuts, drained and sliced
½ cup slivered almonds
½ green pepper, chopped
1 tablespoon grated onion
2 tablespoons chopped pimiento
2 tablespoons white wine
½ teaspoon lemon juice
1 teaspoon salt
1 (10¾-ounce) can cream of chicken soup
½ cup milk
 croutons
1 cup grated Cheddar cheese

1. In a 2-quart bowl, combine turkey, peas, celery, water chestnuts, almonds, green pepper, onion, and pimiento. Sprinkle mixture with wine, lemon juice, and salt; toss gently.

2. In small bowl, blend soup and milk until smooth. Bring to a boil. Pour over casserole and mix well. Cover and cook at 80% power for 5 minutes, stirring halfway through.

3. Cover top of casserole with croutons and sprinkle with cheese. Cook, uncovered, at 70% power for 1½ minutes or until cheese is melted.

Deviled Turkey

SERVES 4 TO 6

2 cups chicken bouillon made from cubes
2 cups herb-flavored packaged dressing
3 cups cooked turkey, cut into bite-size pieces
½ cup water
1 (10-ounce) jar red currant jelly
1 tablespoon prepared mustard
¼ cup relish pickle
2 tablespoons Worcestershire sauce
2 tablespoons butter or margarine

1. Dissolve bouillon cubes in boiling water. Stir into dressing.
2. In a baking dish, make a layer of turkey topped by dressing and repeat once more.
3. Combine remaining ingredients in a 4-cup measure. Cook on High for 2½ minutes, stirring after 1½ minutes.
4. Pour evenly over turkey and dressing.
5. Bake, uncovered, at 80% power for 8 minutes.

Open-faced Turkey Sandwiches

SERVES 4

4 slices buttered toast
4 slices cooked turkey
   salt and pepper
½ cup salad dressing or mayonnaise
2 celery stalks, chopped
¼ cup chopped green onion
1 medium apple, pared and shredded
½ teaspoon curry powder
¼ teaspoon salt
   pepper

1. Place toast on a flat baking dish or platter. Cover with turkey and sprinkle with salt and pepper to taste.

2. Combine salad dressing, celery, onion, apple, curry powder, salt and pepper. Spread one-fourth of mixture on top of each piece of turkey.

3. Cook on High for 4 to 5 minutes.

Rice and Pastas

Noodles with Almonds

½ cup slivered almonds
4 tablespoons butter or margarine, melted
3 tablespoons poppy seeds
1 tablespoon lemon juice
½ teaspoon salt
8 ounces noodles, cooked

1. Sauté almonds in a small amount of butter in a skillet. They should be lightly browned.
2. Combine melted butter, poppy seeds, lemon juice, and salt. Pour over cooked noodles.

Noodles and Mushrooms

1 pound fresh mushrooms, sliced
3 tablespoons butter or margarine
  salt
8 ounces noodles, cooked
2 tablespoons butter or margarine, melted
  parsley

1. Place mushrooms and 3 tablespoons of butter in a baking dish and sauté on High for 2 to 3 minutes, stirring once. Lightly season with salt.
2. Combine noodles and mushrooms and drizzle with melted butter. Reheat if necessary.
3. Sprinkle top with parsley.

Noodles with Mushrooms and Cheese

SERVES 8

1   medium onion, chopped
4   tablespoons butter or margarine
1   pound fresh mushrooms, sliced
1   (8-ounce) package noodles, cooked
1½ cups shredded Cheddar cheese
½   cup milk
2   teaspoons salt
¼   teaspoon pepper
     pinch of dill
     Parmesan cheese

1. Sauté onions in butter on High for 2 to 3 minutes.
2. Add mushrooms and sauté at 70% power for 4 minutes.
3. Combine all ingredients except the Parmesan cheese and stir to mix.
4. Sprinkle the top with Parmesan cheese. Bake at 70% power for 3 minutes or until heated through.

Baked Rice with Cheese

SERVES 6

4 eggs, beaten
1 teaspoon salt
¼ teaspoon dry mustard
2 cups cooked rice
1 cup milk
1 tablespoon butter or margarine
1 cup grated Cheddar cheese

1. Combine eggs, salt, and mustard. Stir in rice.
2. Put milk, butter, and cheese in a bowl and cook at 70% power for 8 to 10 minutes. Pour into a blender and mix at low speed until smooth.
3. Combine all ingredients and mix well. Cook at 70% power for 8 to 10 minutes.
4. Let stand for about 5 minutes to finish cooking.

Red Rice

SERVES 6 TO 8

2 cups cooked rice
3 tablespoons tomato paste
1 onion, chopped
½ green pepper, chopped
¾ teaspoon salt
¼ cup vinegar
⅓ cup oil
1 garlic clove, pressed
¼ teaspoon pepper
½ teaspoon dry mustard

Combine all ingredients and chill for 2 hours. Serve on a bed of lettuce.

Spanish Rice

SERVES 4

3 slices bacon, minced
½ cup raw rice
1 small onion, sliced
1 (14½-ounce) can tomatoes, undrained
½ teaspoon salt
1 teaspoon paprika
½ green pepper, diced
1 garlic clove, pressed

1. Cook bacon in a skillet and remove it from the grease.
2. Brown the rice in the drippings; add onion and stir until brown. Stir in tomatoes, salt, paprika, green pepper, garlic, and bacon.
3. Put mixture in a bowl and cook, covered, on High for 5 minutes. Stir and continue to cook, covered, on 50% power for 28 minutes, stirring every 5 minutes. If it seems to be getting a little dry halfway through, add 1 tablespoon water.

Spaghetti Casserole

SERVES 4

1 pound ground beef
2 medium onions, chopped
1 (10¾-ounce) can tomato soup
1 (6-ounce) can tomato paste
½ cup tomato juice
½ green pepper, chopped
⅛ to ¼ teaspoon pepper
1 tablespoon salt
8 ounces spaghetti
1 (10¾-ounce) can cream of mushroom soup
1 cup fresh mushrooms, sliced
8 ounces Cheddar cheese, grated
  Parmesan cheese

1. Set a plastic colander in a cake dish or pie plate. Put in crumbled ground beef and onions. Cook on High for 3 minutes; stir. Continue to cook on High for 3 more minutes. Set aside. All the grease and extra calories will be in the dish, not the meat.

2. In a large bowl, combine tomato soup, tomato paste, tomato juice, and green pepper. Stir in meat mixture. Cook, covered, on High for 4 minutes, stirring halfway through.

3. Add salt and pepper. Cook, covered, at 50% power for 14 minutes, stirring once halfway through.

4. While sauce is simmering, cook spaghetti on the stove and drain. Place in a 2-quart baking dish; top with mushroom soup and cheese.

5. Add mushrooms to cooked sauce; pour over casserole. Sprinkle with Parmesan cheese.

6. Cook, uncovered, at 50% power for 10 minutes.

Lasagna

SERVES 6 TO 8

1   pound ground beef
½   pound bulk sausage
1   (1½-ounce) package spaghetti sauce mix
1   (16-ounce) can tomato sauce
1   (16-ounce) can tomatoes, chopped
1   cup sliced mushrooms
1½ teaspoons Italian herb seasoning
1   garlic clove, crushed
1   (8-ounce) package lasagna noodles, cooked
1   pound ricotta cheese
1   pound mozzarella cheese, grated

1. Combine beef and sausage in a plastic colander with a glass pie plate underneath. Cook on High for 6 to 8 minutes, stirring every 2 minutes.

2. In a large bowl combine spaghetti sauce mix, tomato sauce, chopped tomatoes and liquid, mushrooms, seasoning, and garlic with the meat. Cover and cook at 70% power for 12 minutes, stirring once.

3. Assemble lasagna in a 3-quart baking dish. Make a layer of noodles topped with sauce, ricotta, and mozzarella. Repeat for two more layers. Bake, uncovered, at 70% power for 15 minutes or until heated through to center.

Fruit

Applesauce

4 cups apples (about 4), pared, cored, and quartered
¼ cups hot water
½ cup sugar
   drop of oil of cinnamon, optional

1. Combine apples, water, and sugar in a round bowl. Cover tightly and cook on High for 5 minutes, stirring once.
2. Process in food processor or blender to desired consistency.
3. Add a drop of oil of cinnamon and stir to blend.
4. Serve warm or chilled.

Baked Apples

SERVES 4

4 cooking apples
   lemon slice or juice
½ cup dark brown sugar, packed firm
½ teaspoon ground cinnamon
⅛ teaspoon ground cloves
½ cup fine-chopped walnuts
¼ cup butter or margarine

1. Wash and core the apples. Peel ¼ to ⅓ the skin off top of apple. Rub pared area with lemon slice or sprinkle with lemon juice.
2. Combine brown sugar, cinnamon, cloves, and walnuts. Cut in butter for crumbly texture. Food processor is ideal for this.
3. Fill center of apples with mixture, packing it firm. Use end of wooden spoon to pack.

4. Place apples in a casserole and sprinkle with remaining mixture.

5. Cover with waxed paper and cook on High for 5 to 6 minutes.

6. Let stand for 5 to 10 minutes to finish cooking.

Cherry Fizz Salad

SERVES 16

1 (16½-ounce) can pitted dark sweet cheeries
1 (20-ounce) can crushed pineapple
1 (3-ounce) package black cherry-flavored gelatin
1 (3-ounce) package raspberry-flavored gelatin
1 (12-ounce) can cola drink
2 (3-ounce) packages cream cheese, softened
2 medium celery stalks, diced fine
1 cup chopped walnuts
½ cup shredded coconut

1. Drain the juice from the cherries and pineapple into a 4-cup measure. If it is not 2 cups of juice, add water to that amount. Bring to a boil on High, about 3 to 4 minutes.

2. Stir in gelatin to dissolve.

3. Stir in cola.

4. Refrigerate until slightly thickened.

5. Cream cheese may be softened in the microwave. Remove cheese from the foil wrapper and allow 15 seconds at 10% power for each piece.

6. In a mixer, beat the cheese until it is fluffy.

7. Add celery, walnuts, and coconut. Stir in cherries, and pineapple.

8. Fold cheese mixture into gelatin.

9. Pour into a 13 × 9 × 2-inch dish and chill until firm.

10. Cut into squares for serving.

Baked Peaches

SERVES 4 TO 6

1 (16-ounce) can peach halves
½ cup brown sugar
¼ teaspoon ground cinnamon
   butter

1. Place peaches in a baking dish.
2. Mix brown sugar and cinnamon and put a portion in the center of each peach half. Dot with butter. Pour juice from can into bottom of dish.
3. Cook on High for 3 to 4 minutes or until butter is melted.
4. Spoon extra sauce from dish over each peach when served.

Pears Poached in Wine

SERVES 4

4 firm pears with stems
4 whole cloves
1 cup red wine
1 cup hot water
½ cup sugar
   peel of 1 lemon, grated

1. Peel pears with a potato peeler, being careful to leave the stem in place.
2. Remove the blossom end and stud with a clove.
3. In a large bowl, combine the wine, water, sugar, and rind. Cook on High for 2 minutes, stirring once.
4. Add pears and cook, covered, on High for 10 minutes, turning the pears over every 3 minutes. Pears should be tender.
5. Serve warm or refrigerate overnight to allow flavor to develop.

Fruit-filled Pineapple

SERVES 4 TO 6

1 fresh pineapple
1 cup shredded coconut
½ cup sliced almonds
1 (11-ounce) can mandarin orange slices, drained
½ cup maraschino cherries, halved
1 banana, sliced
1 cup strawberries or blueberries or raspberries
½ cup orange marmalade
¼ cup rum

1. Cut the pineapple, including the crown, in half lengthwise. Cut out the fruit and leave the shell intact. Chop the fruit into bite-size pieces.

2. Combine all the ingredients and toss together. Fill shells with the mixture. Place in a large baking dish and cover with waxed paper. Cook on High for 4 minutes.

3. Serve warm or chilled. Leftovers will keep in the refrigerator.

Fruit Compote with Wine

1 (20-ounce) can pineapple chunks
2 (11-ounce) cans mandarin orange slices
1 cup pitted prunes
½ cup dry white wine
   brown sugar
1 teaspoon ground cinnamon
¼ teaspoon ground cloves
   peel of 1 orange
   shredded coconut

1. Drain the juice from the pineapple and orange slices but don't throw it away. Save and use in place of water when making flavored gelatin or freeze as a snack for the children.
2. Place pineapple chunks, orange slices, and prunes in a 2-quart bowl.
3. Pour the wine into a 1-cup measure. Add brown sugar to bring the level to one full cup. Stir in cinnamon and cloves. Pour over the fruit.
4. Grate orange peel over bowl of fruit so the fine spray will fall into the bowl and add extra flavor.
5. Cook, covered, on High for 4 minutes, stirring once.
6. Let stand for 5 minutes.
7. Serve in glass stemware or clear bowl and garnish top with shredded coconut.

Vegetables

Asparagus Sunshine

SERVES 4 TO 6

¼ cup butter or margarine
¼ cup all-purpose flour
1½ cups milk
½ teaspoon salt
    dash of white pepper
1   cup cottage cheese
2   (10-ounce) packages frozen asparagus, cooked and
        drained
    toast points
2   hard-cooked eggs, chopped fine

1. In a 4-cup measure, melt butter.
2. Stir in flour. Cook 30 seconds on High. Stir.
3. Gradually add milk; blend well. Stir in salt and pepper. Cook on High for 4 minutes, stirring after every minute, or until thickened.
4. Stir in cottage cheese. Cook at 50% power for 1 minute.
5. Place asparagus on toast points; top with sauce. Sprinkle chopped eggs on top.

Asparagus and Tomatoes

SERVES 4

1 pound fresh asparagus
1 tomato, sliced thin
3 tablespoon grated Parmesan cheese
1 slice bread, made into fine crumbs
1 tablespoon dried minced onion
1 tablespoon dried minced parsley
  seasoned salt to taste
  pepper to taste
4 tablespoons butter or margarine, melted

1. Snap stem ends off asparagus and rinse.
2. Place in a 1½-quart baking dish with tips in the center; cover tightly. If just rinsed, extra water is not necessary. Cook on High for 6 to 8 minutes. Drain water.
3. Rearrange so that tips are on outer edge. Place tomato slices in a row down the center of the asparagus.
4. Combine Parmesan cheese, bread crumbs, onion, parsley, salt and pepper and sprinkle over top of tomatoes and asparagus. Drizzle melted butter over top.
5. Place under the broiler for 5 minutes.
6. Serve hot.

Baked Beans

SERVES 4 TO 6

6 slices bacon, diced and cooked
½ cup catsup
½ cup maple-flavored syrup
1 tablespoon prepared mustard
1 tablespoon dried minced onion
1 (31-ounce) can pork and beans, drained

1. Combine all ingredients in a bowl.
2. Bake at 70% power for 10 minutes, stirring after 5 minutes.

Green Beans Au Gratin

SERVES 6

2   (10-ounce) packages frozen French-style green beans
4   tablespoons butter or margarine
4   tablespoons flour
1   teaspoon salt
⅛   teaspoon dry mustard
1½ cups milk
½   cup grated Cheddar cheese
    Parmesan cheese
    paprika

1. Cook the beans in their boxes on High for about 8 minutes. Drain and set aside.

2. In a 1½-quart bowl, melt butter.

3. Stir in flour, salt, and mustard. Cook on High for 1½ to 2 minutes or until bubbly.

4. Add milk and cook on High for about 4 minutes, stirring once, or until sauce begins to thicken. Remove from oven and add grated cheese, stirring until melted.

5. Add beans to sauce; sprinkle top with Parmesan cheese and paprika for a touch of color. Cook at 70% power for 7 to 8 minutes until heated through.

Green Beans Caesar

SERVES 4 TO 6

1   teaspoon dried minced onion
1   teaspoon sugar
¼ teaspoon salt
1   tablespoon salad oil
1   tablespoon vinegar
1   (16-ounce) can French-style green beans, drained
1   cup croutons
    grated Parmesan cheese

1. Combine onion, sugar, salt, oil, and vinegar in a 1½-quart bowl. Stir to mix.

2. Add green beans and stir to coat with oil mixture.

3. Cover with plastic wrap and cook at 80% power or High for 6 to 8 minutes, stirring once.

4. Remove from oven and stir in croutons. The quality of the croutons will have a lot to do with the overall quality of the dish. They should be crisp and lightly seasoned.

5. Generously sprinkle top with Parmesan cheese.

Swiss-French Beans

SERVES 6

2 (10-ounce) packages frozen French-style green beans
2 tablespoons butter or margarine
1 tablespoon flour
1 teaspoon salt
¼ teaspoon pepper
1 teaspoon sugar
1 teaspoon dried minced onion
1 cup sour cream
1 cup shredded Swiss cheese

1. Cook beans in their boxes on High for 8 minutes. Drain and set aside.

2. In a 1½-quart bowl, melt butter. Stir in flour, salt, pepper, sugar, onion, and sour cream. Blend until smooth.

3. Add beans to the sauce; mix well. Sprinkle cheese on top. Cook at 70% power just long enough to melt cheese, about 1½ minutes.

Goldenrod Beans

SERVES 8 TO 10

3   (10-ounce) packages frozen green beans, cooked and
    drained
1½ tablespoons butter or margarine
2   tablespoons flour
1   teaspoon salt
    dash black pepper
½   cup water
½   cup milk
½   cup mayonnaise
3   hard-cooked eggs

1. In a 4-cup measure melt butter. Stir in flour, salt, and pepper. Stir until smooth and add water; cook on High for 2 minutes. Add milk and mayonnaise. Stir until smooth.

2. Chop the egg whites and blend them into the sauce.

3. Press the yolks through a sieve and reserve.

4. Stir sauce into the green beans. Sprinkle yolks on top.

5. Reheat at 80% power for 3 minutes.

Green Beans and Tomatoes

SERVES 6

2 (10-ounce) boxes frozen green beans
4 slices bacon, chopped
1 small onion, chopped
1 (16-ounce) can tomatoes, drained and quartered
1 tablespoon chopped pimiento
½ teaspoon salt
¼ teaspoon pepper
  cheese-flavored croutons

1. Cook beans in their boxes on High for 7 minutes. Drain.

2. Cook bacon on High for 4 minutes or until crisp. Remove from grease. Put onion in drippings and sauté on High for 1½ minutes. Drain.

3. Combine all ingredients except croutons and mix well. Cover and cook at 80% power for 4 minutes.

Top to bottom:
Dill and Vermouth Squash (p. 170). Corn-filled Tomatoes (p. 173). Glazed Pecan Carrots (p. 155).

4. Spread croutons on top of casserole. Cook, uncovered, at 80% power for 1 minute.

Three-Green Salad

SERVES 6

2 (10-ounce) packages frozen French-style green beans
1 (10-ounce) package frozen chopped broccoli
½ cup chopped onion
1 (8½-ounce) can artichoke hearts, drained and quartered
½ cup buttermilk-style salad dressing mixed with sour cream
     chopped anchovies or chopped bacon

1. Cook beans and broccoli in the boxes on High for 10 to 12 minutes. Drain well.
2. Combine vegetables with onion and artichokes.
3. Mix the buttermilk dressing with sour cream according to package instructions (if milk and mayonnaise are used, it will be thin). Stir into vegetables so that all are well coated.
4. Cover and refrigerate until well chilled. Garnish with anchovies or bacon.

Harvard Beets

SERVES 6

½ cup sugar
½ cup red wine vinegar or plain vinegar
2 tablespoons cornstarch
2 whole cloves
2 (16-ounce) cans cut beets, drained

1. Combine sugar, vinegar, cornstarch, and cloves in a bowl. Cook on High for 2 minutes, stirring after 1 minute. Mixture should boil and thicken. Remove cloves.
2. Add beets to sauce and cook at 80% power for 4 minutes or until heated.

For a special touch, add grated orange peel and a squeeze of orange juice.

Top to bottom:
Black Forest Cheesecake (p. 188). Mint Stick Brownies (p. 179). Rocky Road Squares (p. 198). Cream Puffs (p. 194).

Broccoli Almondine

SERVES 6 TO 8

2 (10-ounce) packages frozen chopped broccoli
2 tablespoons butter or margarine
2 tablespoons flour
1½ cups milk
1 cup grated Cheddar cheese
1 teaspoon salt
¼ teaspoon pepper
¼ to ½ cup slivered almonds
4 slices crisp bacon, crumbled
  croutons

1. Cook broccoli in the boxes on High for 10 to 12 minutes. Drain well.

2. In a 2-quart bowl, melt butter. Stir in flour until smooth. Gradually add milk, stirring until smooth. Add cheese and cook, uncovered, at 70% power for 2 to 3 minutes or until cheese has melted. Season with salt and pepper.

3. Add broccoli to sauce and stir in almonds. Cook, covered, at 70% power for 4 minutes. Gently push outer edge to center and allow soupy portion to flow to the outer edge.

4. Cover top with croutons and sprinkle with bacon. Cook, uncovered, at 70% power for 4 minutes.

Cheesy Broccoli

SERVES 4

1 (10-ounce) package frozen chopped broccoli
1 cup quick-cooking rice
1 (10¾-ounce) can cream of chicken soup
½ cup milk
1 (8-ounce) jar pasturized processed cheese spread
½ tablespoon salt
½ teaspoon pepper
¼ cup chopped onion
½ cup chopped celery
1 (6-ounce) can water chestnuts, drained and sliced

1. Cook broccoli in the box on High for 4 minutes. Drain.

2. In a bowl, combine rice, soup, milk, and cheese. Cook, covered, on High for 2 minutes or until the cheese is melted and blends easily.

3. Combine all the ingredients and cook, covered, on High for 8 minutes, stirring once.

Broccoli-Corn Casserole

SERVES 4 TO 6

1 (10-ounce) package frozen chopped broccoli
1 (17-ounce) can creamed corn
½ cup cracker crumbs
1 egg, beaten
2 tablespoons butter or margarine, melted
1 tablespoon dried minced onion
½ teaspoon salt
¼ teaspoon pepper
   croutons

1. Cook frozen broccoli in the box on High for 6 to 8 minutes. Drain and place in a 1½-quart bowl.

2. Combine broccoli with remaining ingredients except croutons.

3. Cook, uncovered, at 80% power for 6 to 8 minutes, stirring after 3 or 4 minutes.

4. Sprinkle croutons on top and cook at 80% power for 1 minute.

Hot Curried Cabbage

SERVES 8

2 cups boiling water
3 beef bouillon cubes
1 bay leaf
4 whole cloves
½ teaspoon salt
3 to 3½ pounds cabbage, shredded
1 onion, chopped
1 garlic clove, pressed
4 tablespoons butter or margarine
4 tablespoons flour
1 tablespoon curry powder
1 teaspoon salt
  black pepper
1½ cups sour cream

1. In a 3-quart bowl dissolve bouillon in 2 cups boiling water. Add bay leaf, cloves, and ½ teaspoon salt. Cook at 50% power for 5 minutes. Remove bay leaf and cloves.

2. Add cabbage to broth; stir. Cook, covered, on High for 5 minutes, stirring after 3 minutes. Drain, reserving ½ cup of broth.

3. Sauté onion and garlic in butter, 1½ to 2½ minutes. Blend in flour, curry powder, salt, and pepper. Gradually add sour cream and broth. Cook at 50% power for 2½ minutes or until sauce has thickened.

4. Pour sauce over cabbage; stir to coat the cabbage. Cover and cook at 70% power for about 6 minutes, stirring after 3 minutes.

5. Let stand for 5 minutes before serving.

Candied Carrots

SERVES 6

2 pounds carrots, scraped and sliced
½ cup butter or margarine
½ cup canned jellied cranberry sauce
4 tablespoons brown sugar
½ teaspoon salt

1. Place carrots in a bowl with 1 tablespoon water and cover tightly. Cook on High for 8 minutes, stirring once.
2. In a small bowl, combine the remaining ingredients. Cover and cook on High for 2 minutes. Stir with a whisk to make a smooth sauce. Pour over carrots and cover again.
3. Cook on High for 3 minutes, stirring once.

Glazed Pecan Carrots

SERVES 4 to 6

1   pound carrots, scraped
2   tablespoons butter or margarine, melted
¼   cup brown sugar
2   tablespoons cold water
1½ teaspoons cornstarch
⅓   cup pecans, chopped
     peel of 1 orange, grated

1. Chop carrots in ¼-inch pieces. Place in a 1½-quart bowl; add butter and brown sugar. Cook, covered, on High for 8 to 10 minutes, stirring halfway through.
2. Combine water and corstarch; mix until smooth. Stir into carrot mixture.
3. Add pecans and orange peel.
4. Cook, covered, on High for 2 to 4 minutes or until sauce begins to thicken.
5. Stir before serving.

Tangy Mustard Cauliflower

SERVES 4

1 head fresh cauliflower
  salad dressing or mayonnaise
  dried minced onion
  prepared mustard
1 cup shredded Cheddar cheese

1. Place whole cauliflower in a bowl. If it has just been washed, do not add any water. If dry, add 2 tablespoons water. Cover tightly and cook on High for 8 to 12 minutes. Exactly how long will depend on the size of the cauliflower.

2. Combine enough salad dressing to cover the head, enough mustard so that it does not smell like plain salad dressing, and onion to suit your taste. Mix well and spread over top of cauliflower.

3. Sprinkle top with cheese. Cook at 70% power just long enough to melt cheese, about 1½ minutes.

4. The cauliflower will be so tender that you can easily use a spoon to divide it into serving portions.

Baked Swiss Cauliflower

SERVES 6

1   large head fresh cauliflower
¾   cup bread crumbs
2¾ cups shredded Swiss cheese
1   pint half-and-half
3   egg yolks, beaten
¼   teaspoon ground nutmeg
½   teaspoon salt
¼   teaspoon white pepper
½   cup butter or margarine, melted

1. Break cauliflower into flowerets. Place in a 1½- or 2-quart bowl. Add 1 tablespoon water and cover tightly. Cook on High for 6 to 8 minutes, stirring once halfway through.

2. Combine remaining ingredients except for butter. Pour over cooked cauliflower. Drizzle melted butter over top.

3. Cook, uncovered, at 70% power for 3 to 4 minutes.

4. Let stand for 5 minutes before serving.

Creole Cauliflower

SERVES 4 TO 6

1 head fresh cauliflower or 1 (10-ounce) package frozen
   cauliflower
4 slices bacon, chopped
1 small onion, chopped
1 (8-ounce) can tomato sauce
   pinch of basil
1 teaspoon Worcestershire sauce
   salt and pepper to taste

1. Break the head into flowerets and put in a bowl with 2 tablespoons of water. If using the frozen, add no water. Cover tightly and cook on High for 8 to 10 minutes or until tender, stirring once.

2. Cook bacon and onion together on High for 5 minutes. Drain.

3. Stir in tomato sauce, basil, Worcestershire, and salt and pepper to taste. Pour over cauliflower and return to oven just long enough to heat through.

Chilled Corn Salad

SERVES 4 TO 6

2 (17-ounce) cans corn, drained
½ cup chopped onion
½ cup chopped green pepper
1 tablespoon chopped pimiento
1 tablespoon minced parsley
3 tablespoons tarragon vinegar
1½ tablespoons oil
½ teaspoon salt
¼ teaspoon pepper

Combine all ingredients and chill for several hours. Serve on a bed of raw spinach for added color.

No cooking at all is required for this recipe. But it is a perfectly delicious side dish to prepare on an evening when the microwave oven is being used for a slow-cooking recipe.

Corn Pudding

SERVES 4

2 (17-ounce) cans corn, drained
2 eggs, beaten
¾ cup milk
½ cup sugar
½ teaspoon salt

1. Combine eggs, milk, sugar, and salt in a 1½-quart bowl.
2. Stir in corn.
3. Cook at 70% power for 16 to 18 minutes. Stirring at 4-minute intervals is important if the center portion is to set up.
4. The dish may still be a bit soupy but will continue to set up during a 5-minute standing time.

Philadelphia Corn

SERVES 4

1 (3-ounce) package cream cheese with chives
3 tablespoons milk
1 tablespoon butter or margarine
1 (17-ounce) can corn, drained
½ teaspoon salt

1. Combine cheese, milk, and butter in a blender or food processor and blend until smooth.
2. Combine cheese sauce, corn, and salt in a bowl. Cover and cook at 70% power for 6 minutes, stirring once.

Scalloped Corn and Tomatoes

SERVES 6

1 (17-ounce) can corn, drained
1 (14½-ounce) can tomatoes, undrained and quartered
1 tablespoon sugar
½ teaspoon salt
⅛ teaspoon pepper
6 slices bread, cubed
3 tablespoons butter or margarine, melted

1. Combine all ingredients in a bowl and mix well.
2. Cover and cook at 80% power for 6 to 7 minutes, stirring once.

Hearty Ham and Corn

SERVES 6 to 8

1 small onion, chopped
½ green pepper, chopped
1 cup chopped cooked ham
1 tablespoon butter or margarine
1 (8-ounce) can tomato sauce
½ teaspoon sugar
½ teaspoon salt
  pepper
2 (17-ounce) cans corn, drained

1. Sauté onion, green pepper, and ham in butter, covered, at 70% power for 4 minutes, stirring once.
2. Stir in tomato sauce, sugar, salt, and pepper. Blend well.
3. Stir in corn. Cover and heat at 80% power for 4 to 6 minutes or until heated through.

Peas with Basil

SERVES 4

1   (10-ounce) package frozen peas
2   tablespoons butter or margarine
¼   cup sliced green onions
1½ teaspoons dried parsley
½   teaspoon sugar
½   teaspoon salt
¼   teaspoon basil
    pepper

1. Cook peas in the box on High for 6 minutes.
2. Sauté onions in butter on High for 1½ minutes.
3. Combine all ingredients and stir to mix well. Cook, covered, on High for 2½ minutes or until heated through.

Oriental Peas

SERVES 6

1 (16-ounce) package frozen peas
1 (10¾-ounce) can cream of mushroom soup
1 small can water chestnuts, drained and sliced
1 (16-ounce) can bean sprouts, drained
½ to 1 pound mushrooms, sautéed in butter
1 tablespoon soy sauce

1. Cook peas and drain.
2. Beat soup with a fork. Combine all ingredients and stir.
3. Cook, covered, on 80% power for 8 minutes, stirring every 3 minutes.
4. Let stand for 5 minutes before serving.

Peas and Pastry

SERVES 6

1 cup sliced fresh mushrooms
2 tablespoons butter or margarine
4 slices bacon, diced
1 tablespoon chopped onion
1 tablespoon flour
1 cup half-and-half
1 (17-ounce) can small peas, drained
6 baked patty shells

1. Melt butter in a small baking dish. Add mushrooms and sauté at 70% power for 1½ minutes, stirring once. Set aside.

2. In a 4-cup measure, cook bacon on High for 3 minutes. Do not drain grease. Add onions and sauté on High for about 30 seconds or until tender.

3. Stir flour and half-and-half into measuring cup. Cook on high for 1½ minutes, stirring once, or until bubbly. If sauce lumps, but it in a blender at very low speed.

4. Combine all ingredients except patty shells and cook, covered, at 80% power for 4 minutes, stirring once.

5. Spoon into patty shells.

Vegetable Platter

SERVES 6

3 medium potatoes, baked
1 head broccoli, cut into flowerets
1 head cauliflower, cut into flowerets
1 (16-ounce) can baby carrots, drained
1½ tablespoons butter or margarine, melted
   salt
   pepper
⅓ cup chopped green onions
8 to 12 ounces mozzarella cheese, shredded
   toasted shelled sunflower seeds

1. Slice unpeeled potatoes into rounds, discarding end pieces, and arrange on a large platter.

2. Place broccoli and cauliflower in a bowl with 2 tablespoons water. Cover tightly and cook on High for 10 minutes, stirring once.

3. Place carrots in a bowl and heat, covered, at 80% power for 3 to 4 minutes, stirring once.

4. Cover potatoes with broccoli, cauliflower, and carrots.

5. Drizzle top with melted butter and season lightly with salt and pepper.

6. Sprinkle top with onions.

7. Spread shredded cheese over top. Cook at 70% power until cheese has melted.

8. Sprinkle top with sunflower seeds.

Extra-Special Stuffed Potatoes

SERVES 4

2 large baking potatoes
4 slices of bacon, cooked and crumbled
2 teaspoons dried chives
1 teaspoon dried minced onion
2 tablespoons grated Parmesan cheese
½ cup sour cream
½ teaspoon salt
¼ teaspoon pepper
  paprika

1. Bake the potatoes, and when cool to the touch, scoop out the pulp. Be careful not to tear the shells.

2. Mash the pulp.

3. Mix in all the remaining ingredients except paprika. Blend well. The mixture will look dry. If it tastes dry add more sour cream.

4. Spoon back into the shells and sprinkle top with paprika.

5. Reheat at 80% power. How long will depend on how cool the potatoes were before being scooped out.

Twice-Baked Potatoes

SERVES 2

1 medium-size baking potato
  milk
  butter or margarine
  salt and pepper
  chives (optional)
1 slice cheese

1. Bake potato on High for about 4 minutes. Let stand until cool enough to work with.

2. Cut potato in half and scoop out, leaving skin intact.

3. Mash the potato with milk, butter, salt, and pepper to taste, just as for mashed potatoes. Add chopped chives.

4. Spoon mashed potatoes back into skins. Top each with half a slice of cheese. Bake at 70% power just long enough for cheese to melt.

5. Extras store well in the refrigerator.

St. Pat's Irish Potatoes

SERVES 4 to 6

3 cups mashed potatoes, seasoned
½ cup sour cream
½ teaspoon onion powder
¼ teaspoon seasoned salt
⅛ teaspoon white pepper
1 (10-ounce) package frozen chopped broccoli, cooked and
    drained
1 cup shredded Cheddar cheese
1 cup croutons or fried onion rings

1. Combine potatoes, sour cream, seasonings, and broccoli; mix well.

2. Place half the mixture in bowl; sprinkle with half the cheese; cover with remaining potato mixture.

3. Cook, covered, at 70% power for 4 to 5 minutes. Sprinkle with remaining cheese and croutons or onion rings. Cook, uncovered, at 70% power for 1 to 1½ minutes.

Potatoes Au Gratin

SERVES 6

4 tablespoons butter or margarine, melted
4 tablespoons flour
2 cups milk
½ teaspoon salt, seasoned or plain
2 cups shredded Cheddar cheese
4 medium-size potatoes, peeled and sliced
1 cup bread crumbs
4 tablespoons butter or margarine

1. Stir flour into melted butter. Gradually add milk and stir until smooth. Cook on High for 4 minutes, stirring twice. Add salt.

2. Add cheese to hot sauce and stir until melted.

3. Place potatoes in a large casserole and pour sauce over top. Cook, covered, at 70% power for 26 to 28 minutes, stirring every 6 minutes.

4. On the stove, cook the bread crumbs in butter until golden brown. Sprinkle on top of potatoes.

5. Let stand for 5 minutes before serving.

Potatoes Lancer

SERVES 4 TO 8

5 or 6 potatoes, peeled and coarse-shredded
½ cup hot water
¼ cup butter or margarine
1 cup sour cream
8 ounces Cheddar cheese, shredded
1 tablespoon dried minced onion
1 teaspoon salt
¼ teaspoon pepper
   paprika

1. Place potatoes and water in a 3-quart bowl and cover tightly with plastic wrap. Cook on High for 12 to 14 minutes, stirring every 4 minutes.

2. Pour potatoes into a colander and rinse with hot water. If the bowl has a starchy residue left in it, clean it out.

3. In a 2-quart bowl, combine the butter, sour cream, and Cheddar cheese. Reserve a small portion of the cheese to top the dish with later. Cook at 50% power for 3½ minutes, stirring after 2 minutes.

4. Stir onion, salt, and pepper into cheese mixture.

5. Using the 3-quart bowl, combine the potatoes and cheese mixture. Stir until the potatoes are well coated with the cheese.

6. Sprinkle the top with reserved cheese and paprika. Put in the oven at 70% power for 1½ minutes or until cheese has melted.

Potato Salad

SERVES 4

3 potatoes, peeled
½ cup hot water
¼ cup (or more) chopped gherkin pickles
   or pickled watermelon rind
1 small onion, chopped
½ cup salad dressing or mayonnaise
½ cup sour cream
½ to ¾ teaspoon salt
¼ (generous) teaspoon pepper

1. Slice the potatoes into bite-size pieces. Place in a 2-quart bowl and add hot water. Cover tightly with plastic wrap and cook on High for 12 minutes, stirring once.

2. Rinse potatoes to remove starchy residue.

3. Cool slightly.

4. Stir in pickles and onions.

5. Combine salad dressing or mayonnaise, sour cream, salt and pepper; blend well. Stir into potatoes.

6. Chill.

Sweet Potatoes and Apples in the Shell

SERVES 4 TO 6

4 medium-size sweet potatoes
2 tablespoons butter or margarine, melted
1 teaspoon grated orange peel
½ teaspoon salt
2 tablespoons brown sugar
2 tablespoons orange juice
½ teaspoon cinnamon
1 apple, pared and chopped

1. Pierce the potatoes with a fork and bake on High for about 16 minutes.
2. Combine the butter, orange peel, salt, brown sugar, orange juice, and cinnamon.
3. Cut the baked potatoes in half. Scoop out the potato and add to sugar mixture. With an electric mixer, beat until smooth and fluffy. Stir in the apple.
4. Spoon the mixture back into the shells and place in a baking dish or on a platter. Cook, covered, on High for 4 minutes.

Sweet Potatoes in Orange Cups

SERVES 6

3 large oranges, halved
1 (1-pound 13-ounce) can sweet potatoes, drained
3 tablespoons butter or margarine, melted
½ cup brown sugar, packed firm
1 teaspoon salt
1 teaspoon ground cinnamon
2 tablespoons brown sugar

1. Remove the pulp from the orange halves, chop fine, and set aside.
2. Drain the sweet potatoes and mash.
3. Combine potatoes, orange pulp, butter, ½ cup brown sugar, and salt. Mix well and spoon back into the orange cups.

4. Combine cinnamon and 2 tablespoons brown sugar. Sprinkle on top of each orange cup.

5. Cook at 80% power for 8 minutes.

Sweet Potato Fantasy

SERVES 6

1 (17-ounce) can sweet potatoes
1 (8¼-ounce) can crushed pineapple; reserve juice
1 apple, peeled and diced
1 (8½-ounce) can water chestnuts, sliced
1 (8¼-ounce) can pineapple rings; reserve juice
1 tablespoon butter
⅓ cup sugar
½ teaspoon ground cinnamon
¼ teaspoon ground ginger
3 tablespoons rum

1. In a mixing bowl, mash the sweet potatoes.

2. Stir in the crushed pineapple, apple, and water chestnuts.

3. In a 4-cup measure, melt the butter. Stir in sugar to form a paste. Add cinnamon, ginger, rum, and reserved pineapple juice from both cans. Bring to a boil on High, about 1 or 2 minutes. Boil for 1 minute.

4. Stir half the syrup into the sweet potato mixture and blend well.

5. Line the bottom of a 1½-quart bowl with the pineapple rings.

6. Pour the sweet potato mixture on top of the rings. Pour remaining half of syrup on top.

7. Bake, uncovered, on an inverted pie plate or saucer, for 10 minutes at 80% power.

8. Let stand for 5 minutes before serving.

Polynesian Casserole

SERVES 4

1 (1-pound 13-ounce) can sweet potatoes, drained and sliced
1 banana, sliced
1 (8¾-ounce) can crushed pineapple
  salt
  flaked coconut

1. Arrange sweet potatoes and banana slices in a 1½-quart bowl.

2. Spread crushed pineapple on top and pour juice over all. Be sure bananas are moistened so they will not discolor.

3. Sprinkle lightly with salt.

4. Sprinkle top with coconut.

5. Cover and cook at 60% power for 6 to 8 minutes.

Spinach Supreme

SERVES 4 TO 6

2 (10-ounce) packages frozen chopped spinach, cooked and
    drained
4 slices bacon, cooked and crumbled
1 (2½-ounce) jar mushroom slices
  dash of white pepper
½ cup sour cream
1 cup shredded Cheddar cheese

1. Place cooked spinach in a bowl.

2. Top with a layer of the bacon and then the mushrooms. Add pepper. Cover and heat at 80% power for 4 minutes or until warm through.

3. Top with sour cream and cheese. Bake uncovered at 70% power just long enough to melt the cheese.

Spinach Ring

SERVES 6

2 (10-ounce) packages frozen spinach, cooked and drained
¼ cup half-and-half or milk
4 eggs, beaten
1 teaspoon sugar
½ teaspoon salt

1. Combine spinach and milk and cook on High for 1 minute.
2. Stir in remaining ingredients and mix well.
3. Pour spinach mixture into a 1½-quart ring mold. Cook at 70% power for 6 minutes.
4. Let stand for 5 minutes before serving.

Yellow Squash Casserole

SERVES 4 TO 6

4 yellow (summer) squash
¼ cup chopped onion
½ cup sour cream
¼ teaspoon salt
    dash pepper
    dash of dried basil

Topping:

1 slice of bread, crumbed
½ cup shredded Cheddar cheese
4 slices bacon, cooked and crumbled
¼ cup butter or margarine, melted
    paprika

1. Combine topping ingredients and set aside.
2. Slice squash into thin rounds and place in a bowl with 2 tablespoons of water and the chopped onion. Cover tightly with plastic wrap and cook on High for 6 minutes, stirring once, or until tender. Drain liquid.

3. Place squash, onion, sour cream, salt, pepper, and basil in a food processor or blender and process until smooth.

4. Pour into a small baking dish. Cover with topping. Bake at 70% power for 6 to 8 minutes or until heated through and cheese has melted.

Dill and Vermouth Squash

SERVES 4

1 teaspoon dill weed
⅔ cup dry white vermouth
2 tablespoons butter or margarine
2 medium zucchini, sliced
3 medium yellow (summer) squash, sliced
1 medium onion, chopped
2 tomatoes, quartered
  Parmesan cheese

1. In a 2-quart baking dish, combine dill, vermouth, and butter. Cook, covered, on High for 2 to 3 minutes.

2. In same dish, combine remaining ingredients. Cook, covered, on High for 8 minutes, stirring every 3 minutes.

3. Sprinkle top with Parmesan cheese, salt and pepper to taste.

4. Let stand for 5 minutes to complete cooking.

Zucchini Au Gratin

SERVES 4 TO 6

2 pounds zucchini, sliced
¼ cup chopped onion
¼ cup butter or margarine
2½ tablespoons flour
1 teaspoon salt
⅛ teaspoon ground allspice
   pinch cayenne pepper
   pinch white pepper
1¼ cups milk
2 tablespoons grated Parmesan cheese
1 cup grated Swiss cheese

1. Cook zucchini with 2 tablespoons of water, covered, on High for 3 to 4 minutes. Drain, rinse in cold water, and drain again. Set aside.

2. Sauté the onion in butter on High for 2 to 4 minutes.

3. Stir in flour, salt, allspice, cayenne, pepper, and milk. Cook on High for 5 minutes or until bubbly.

4. Stir in Parmesan cheese. Add zucchini and cook, covered, at 70% power for 6 minutes.

5. Sprinkle top with Swiss cheese and cook at 70% power for 2 minutes.

Stuffed Zucchini Boats

SERVES 4

2 large zucchini
   salt
1 tablespoon butter or margarine
½ pound mushrooms, chopped
½ cup chopped ham or pepperoni
2 slices bread, crumbed
½ teaspoon salt
¼ teaspoon pepper
   shredded Swiss cheese

1. Split zucchini in half and scoop out the pulp, leaving shells intact. A grapefruit spoon works well for this task.

2. Lightly sprinkle the shells with salt and place upside down on a paper towel to drain.

3. Chop the pulp. Place in a bowl with butter and sauté, covered, on High for 3 minutes, stirring once.

4. Add mushrooms, cover, and cook on High for 1 minute, stirring once.

5. Stir in ham, bread crumbs, salt, and pepper. Fill shells with mixture.

6. Place stuffed shells in a baking dish, cover tightly with plastic wrap, and cook on High for 3 minutes.

7. Rearrange shells for even cooking.

8. Sprinkle top with shredded cheese and cook, uncovered, at 70% power for 3 minutes or until cheese has melted.

9. Watch the time carefully because the zucchini size can vary greatly.

Stuffed Tomatoes

SERVES 6

6   tomatoes
1½ cups small croutons
½   cup shredded Cheddar cheese
3   slices bacon, cooked and crumbled
    or ¼ to ½ cup fine-diced cooked ham
4   tablespoons butter or margarine, melted
    salt and pepper to taste
    parsley for garnish

1. Cut a slice off the stem end of each tomato and discard. With a knife or a grapefruit spoon, carefully scoop out the seeds and pulp, leaving a fairly thick wall. Turn the tomatoes cut side down on a piece of paper toweling and allow to drain for several minutes. Chop the pulp and place it in a bowl.

2. To the pulp, add the croutons, cheese, bacon, and melted butter. Mix well. Add salt and pepper to taste.

3. Fill the center of each tomato with a portion of the mixture. Bake at 70% power for 6 to 8 minutes.

4. Garnish with a sprig of parsley or serve on a platter with a bed of leafy lettuce.

Corn-filled Tomatoes

SERVES 4 TO 6

4 large or 6 medium tomatoes
1 (17-ounce) can corn, drained
1 tablespoon dried minced onion
1 teaspoon dried parsley, minced
   (or 1 tablespoon fresh parsley, minced)
1 teaspoon salt
¼ teaspoon pepper
2 slices bread, crumbed
4 tablespoons butter or margarine, melted
   fresh parsley, optional

1. Cut a slice off the stem end of each tomato and discard. With a knife or a grapefruit spoon, carefully scoop out the seeds and pulp, leaving a fairly thick wall. Turn the tomatoes cut side down on a piece of paper toweling and allow to drain while the remaining ingredients are prepared.

2. In a small bowl, toss together the corn, onion, parsley, salt, pepper, bread crumbs, and melted butter. Fill each tomato with a portion of the mixture.

3. Arrange the tomatoes in a baking dish or on a platter, leaving space around each one. Bake, uncovered, on High for 4 to 6 minutes. Garnish with fresh parsley. Serve at once.

Tomato Pie

SERVES 6

2 large tomatoes, sliced
  salt and pepper
  flour
2 tablespoons oil
½ cup chopped green onions
¼ to ½ cup chopped ripe olives or green olives
1 baked pie shell
½ to 1 cup grated provolone cheese
2 eggs, beaten
1 cup shredded Cheddar cheese
1 cup evaporated milk

1. Sprinkle tomato slices with salt and pepper. Coat both sides with flour. Sauté in hot oil until lightly browned (on the stove).

2. Set aside 1 tablespoon on onion and sprinkle remaining onion and olives in pie shell. Top with provolone cheese and tomato slices.

3. Combine eggs, Cheddar cheese, and evaporated milk; mix well. Pour over tomatoes and cook at 70% power for 14 minutes.

4. Sprinkle top with remaining onion and let stand for 5 minutes before serving.

Desserts

Apple Brown Betty

SERVES 4

4 large cooking apples, pared and sliced thin
1 cup sugar
¼ teaspoon ground cloves
¼ teaspoon ground cinnamon
¼ teaspoon salt
3 cups soft bread crumbs
4 tablespoons butter or margarine, melted

1. Combine sugar, spices, and salt; set aside.
2. In a 2-quart bowl, build layers of bread crumbs, apples, and a sprinkling of sugar. Repeat until all ingredients are used. Pour melted butter on top.
3. Cook, covered, on High for 8 to 10 minutes.
4. Let stand for 5 to 10 minutes before serving.
5. Extra good with a dollop of hard sauce melting over the top.

175

Cherry Bread-and-Butter Pudding

SERVES 4

12 slices white bread
    butter or margarine, softened
    powdered cinnamon
1 (16-ounce) jar cherry preserves
4 eggs, beaten
2⅓ cups milk
2 tablespoons sugar

1. Spread each slice of bread with butter. Trim crust.
2. Grease an 8 × 8-inch dish. Arrange four slices of bread in bottom of dish. Sprinkle lightly with cinnamon. Spread a spoonful of preserves on each slice. Repeat, making two more layers.
3. In medium-size bowl, combine beaten eggs, milk, and sugar. Mix well. Pour over bread.
4. Cook, covered, on 70% power for 8 to 10 minutes, rotating dish after 4 minutes.
5. Serve warm.

Plum Cobbler

SERVES 6

4 cups (about 1¾ pounds) plums, pitted and quartered
1½ cups sugar
¼ cup water
2 tablespoons quick-cooking tapioca
2 tablespoons butter or margarine
1½ cups biscuit mix
2 tablespoons sugar
⅓ cup milk
2 tablespoons butter or margarine, melted
    sugar

1. Combine plums, 1½ cups sugar, water, and tapioca. Cook, covered, on High for 7 minutes, stirring once.

2. Add 2 tablespoons butter and stir until melted.

3. Combine biscuit mix, 2 tablespoons sugar, milk, and melted butter. Stir just until moistened. Drop by spoonfuls on top of plum mixture.

4. Bake, in a conventional oven, at 425° for 20 minutes. Remove from oven and sprinkle top with sugar.

Danish Almond Rice

SERVES 6

¼ cup raw rice
2¼ cups milk
¼ cup sugar
¼ teaspoon salt
1 teaspoon vanilla
¼ teaspoon almond extract
1 cup heavy cream
1 tablespoon confectioners' sugar
¼ cup toasted slivered almonds
1 can cherry pie filling

1. Rinse the rice with hot water.

2. In large bowl, bring milk to a boil (about 5 to 6 minutes if milk is cold).

3. Stir in rice; reduce setting to 50% power and cook, covered, for 20 to 25 minutes, stirring every 5 minutes. Set aside and let stand, covered, until all the milk is absorbed.

4. Stir in sugar, salt, vanilla, and almond extract. Cover and chill.

5. Just before serving, whip the cream and powdered sugar until stiff. Fold into pudding along with the almonds.

6. Pour into individual cups and top with a spoonful or two of cherry pie filling.

Supermoist Chocolate Brownies

YIELD: 1 RING MOLD

½ cup butter, softened
¾ cup dark brown sugar, packed firm
1 egg
1 teaspoon vanilla
½ cup chocolate syrup
1 tablespoon cocoa
1 cup all-purpose flour
⅛ teaspoon baking powder
1 cup chopped walnuts

1. In a mixer, beat the butter, sugar, egg, and vanilla until creamy.
2. Blend in chocolate syrup and cocoa.
3. In a 1-cup measure, combine the flour and baking powder. Blend in with the chocolate mixture. Beat no longer than necessary to moisten all ingredients.
4. Stir in walnuts.
5. Spread batter evenly in a ring mold or glass cake dish with an inverted glass in the center.
6. Bake at 60% power for 5 to 6 minutes, rotating dish once. Continue baking on High for 3 minutes.
7. Portions of the top may still be moist after cooking. If the brownies are pulling away from the edge, they will finish cooking during the standing time.
8. Do not cut until completely cooled.

Mint Stick Brownies

YIELD: 1 RING MOLD

Brownies:

2 squares unsweetened chocolate
½ cup butter or margarine
2 eggs, beaten
1 cup sugar
½ cup all-purpose flour
¼ teaspoon peppermint flavoring
⅛ teaspoon salt

Mint Frosting:

1 cup confectioners' sugar
2 tablespoons butter or margarine, softened
1 tablespoon milk
½ teaspoon peppermint flavoring
 drop of green food coloring

Glaze Topping:

1 square unsweetened chocolate
1 tablespoon butter or margarine

1. Combine chocolate and butter for brownies in a bowl. Melt at 50% power for about 3½ minutes.
2. Combine eggs, sugar, flour, peppermint, and salt. Stir in chocolate and butter; blend well. Pour into a ring mold. Bake at 60% power for 6 minutes and on High for 3 minutes. Let cool completely.
3. Combine frosting ingredients and mix until creamy. Spread on cooled brownies. Refrigerate while making glaze.
4. Melt chocolate and butter for glaze at 50% power for 2 minutes. Spread over frosting. Refrigerate until set.

Golden Girl Brownies

YIELD: ONE 8-INCH CAKE DISH

Brownies:

½ cup butter or margarine, melted
1 cup brown sugar, lightly packed
2 eggs
1 cup all-purpose flour
⅛ teaspoon baking powder
½ teaspoon vanilla
1 cup chopped nuts

Topping:

½ cup brown sugar, lightly packed
1 tablespoon milk
1 tablespoon butter or margarine
1½ teaspoons all-purpose flour
   pinch of salt
¼ teaspoon vanilla

1. With a mixer, combine melted butter, 1 cup brown sugar, and eggs. Blend until smooth and creamy.

2. Add flour, baking powder, and vanilla. Mix just until all ingredients are moistened.

3. Stir in chopped nuts.

4. Put batter into an 8-inch cake dish and smooth to distribute evenly.

5. Set on top of an inverted pie plate and bake at 60% power for 6 minutes, rotating dish once. Continue to bake on High for 2½ to 3 minutes.

6. Combine all ingredients for topping in a 4-cup measure. Cook on High for 1½ minutes or until boiling. Stir. Allow to boil on High for 1 minute.

7. Pour topping over warm cake and spread evenly.

8. Let stand until topping is set.

Gingerbread

YIELD: ONE RING MOLD

¼ cup butter or margarine
½ cup sugar
1 egg
¼ cup boiling water
½ cup molasses
1¼ cup all-purpose flour
½ teaspoon baking soda
⅛ teaspoon salt
1 teaspoon ginger
½ teaspoon ground cinnamon

1. With a mixer, cream butter, sugar, and egg.
2. Gradually add boiling water.
3. Add molasses; blend well.
4. Add flour, baking soda, salt, ginger, and cinnamon. Mix only until all ingredients are moistened.
5. Pour into a ring mold and spread mixture evenly.
6. Bake at 60% power for 5½ to 6 minutes, rotating dish once. Continue to bake on High for 2½ to 3 minutes.
7. Let stand for 5 minutes on a flat surface.
8. Serve with lemon sauce, hard sauce, or whipped cream.

Chocolate Fudge Pudding Cake

SERVES 6

1 cup all-purpose flour
1½ teaspoons baking powder
¼ teaspoon salt
¾ cup sugar
2 tablespoons cocoa

½ cup milk
2 tablespoons butter or margarine, melted

1 cup brown sugar
4 tablespoons cocoa

1¼ cups hot water

1. Combine first five ingredients in a mixing bowl.
2. Stir in the next two ingredients.
3. Spread the mixture in a ring mold.
4. Sprinkle top with mixture of brown sugar and cocoa.
5. Pour hot water over top of batter.
6. This will run over the side of the dish, so line the bottom of the oven with paper towels.
7. Cook on High for 5 minutes. Rotate the dish and cook on High for 5 more minutes.
8. Let stand for 5 to 10 minutes. Best served warm.

Mississippi Mud Cake

YIELD: ONE 8- OR 9-INCH CAKE

½ cup butter or margarine
¼ cup cocoa
2 eggs, beaten
1 cup sugar
¾ cup all-purpose flour
1 cup mini-marshmallows

Frosting:

¼ cup butter or margarine
1½ tablespoons cocoa
1 tablespoon light corn syrup
1 cup confectioners' sugar
1½ tablespoons milk
¼ to ½ cup chopped pecans

1. Combine ½ cup butter and ¼ cup cocoa in glass 1-cup measure. Cook on High for 1 to 1½ minutes or until melted; stir.
2. In a medium-size bowl, combine melted butter and cocoa with eggs, 1 cup sugar, and flour, stirring to mix. Pour into ungreased cake dish; cook on High for 6 to 7 minutes, rotating dish after 3 minutes. It should still look wet on top.
3. Evenly distribute marshamallows on top of cake. Cook on High just long enough to melt marshmallows. They will look puffy but will not lose their shape. Spread to cover top.

4. Let cake cool completely, about 30 minutes.

5. Combine ¼ cup butter and 1½ tablespoons cocoa; cook on High until melted, about 1 minute. Add corn syrup and confectioners' sugar; stir until smooth. Gradually add 1½ tablespoons milk. Stir in pecans. Spread over top of cake.

Carrot Cake

YIELD: TWO 8- OR 9-INCH LAYERS

2 cups sugar
1½ cups oil
4 eggs, beaten
2 cups all-purpose flour
1 teaspoon salt
1 teaspoon baking soda
2 teaspoons ground cinnamon
½ cup chopped walnuts
3 cups grated carrots

Cream Cheese Icing:

½ cup butter, softened
1 (8-ounce) package cream cheese, softened
1 (1-pound) box confectioners' sugar
2 teaspoons vanilla

1. Combine sugar, oil, and eggs together in electric mixer bowl.

2. Gradually add flour, salt, soda, and cinnamon.

3. Fold in nuts and carrots.

4. Line the bottom of a cake dish with waxed paper. Bake one layer at a time. Bake at 50% power for 7 minutes and on High for 3 minutes. Let stand for 10 minutes. If any moisture remains on the top, blot it off with a paper towel.

5. With an electric mixer, cream together the butter and cream cheese. Add powdered sugar and vanilla. Beat well. Spread on completely cooled cake. Top with sprinkling of chopped nuts if desired.

Strawberry Cake

YIELD: TWO 8- OR 9-INCH LAYERS

1 box white cake mix, 2-layer size
3 tablespoons all-purpose flour
1 (3-ounce) box strawberry gelatin
1 cup vegetable oil
¼ cup water
4 eggs, beaten
2 cups strawberries

Icing:

½ cup butter or margarine, softened
1 (1-pound) box confectioners' sugar
1 cup strawberries

1. Combine cake mix, flour, and gelatin. Add oil, water, and eggs.

2. Purée strawberries in blender or food processor; add to mixture.

3. Line bottom of two cake dishes with waxed paper; grease paper. Pour in cake mix.

4. Bake one layer at a time at 60% power for 6 to 7 minutes, rotating dish after 4 minutes. Cook on High for 2 to 3 minutes, rotating dish halfway through.

5. Completely cool cake.

6. Combine icing ingredients and mix until smooth. Spread between layers, on sides and top.

Chocolate Cake

YIELD: 2 LAYERS

1½ cups sugar
¾ cup butter or margarine, softened
4   eggs
¾ cup milk, room temperature
1   teaspoon vanilla
2   cups all-purpose flour
¾ teaspoon soda
½ teaspoon salt
¾ cup cocoa

1. Cream the butter and sugar with an electric mixer.

2. Add eggs to creamed mixture one at a time, beating well after each addition.

3. Add milk gradually.

4. Add vanilla.

5. Combine the flour, soda, salt, and cocoa. By hand, blend in with the other ingredients. If the mixer is used for this step, keep it on the lowest speed.

6. Line the bottom of a glass cake pan with waxed paper. After the batter has rested for 10 minutes, pour half into the dish. Bake at 60% power for 5 to 6 minutes, rotating once. Continue to bake on High for 2½ to 3 minutes, rotating once. Let cake stand on a flat surface for 10 minutes before removing from dish. Repeat with remaining half of batter.

7. This cake does not tend to pull away from the edge of the dish. Carefully run a sharp knife between the edge of the cake and the dish before turning out. There may also be a small wet spot in the center of the bottom surface. Gently scrape the moisture off or blot with a paper towel. Additional cooking would dry out the cake.

8. Frost when completely cooled. Store in an airtight container because there is no crust to prevent the cake from drying out.

Chocolate Fudge Icing

YIELD: FROSTING FOR A TWO-LAYER CAKE

½ cup butter or margarine
¾ cup cocoa
2¾ cups confectioners' sugar
⅓ cup milk
1   teaspoon vanilla

1. Melt butter.

2. Stir in cocoa and cook on High for about 1½ minutes or until mixture reaches a boil, stirring once. Cool completely.

3. Combine all ingredients in an electric mixer and blend until smooth. If mixture is too thin, add more sugar. If too thick, add small amount of milk.

Penuche Icing

YIELD: ENOUGH FROSTING FOR A 2-LAYER CAKE

½ cup butter
1   cup light brown sugar, packed firm
¼ cup milk
1¾ to 2 cups confectioners' sugar, sifted

1. In a 1½-quart bowl, melt the butter.

2. Stir in brown sugar. Return to oven and cook on High for 2 minutes or until boiling.

3. Add milk and return to oven on High for 1 minute.

4. Place the bowl in a dish of ice cubes and allow the mix to cool to the touch.

5. Gradually stir in the confectioners' sugar, leaving the bowl surrounded by ice cubes. If you skip sifting the sugar, it will take more effort to stir out the lumps.

6. Stir until spreading consistency is reached. If too thin, add more confectioners' sugar; if too thick, add a little more milk.

Chocolate Cheesecake

SERVES 8

Crust:

3 tablespoons butter or margarine
1 ½ cups chocolate wafer cookie crumbs
2 tablespoons sugar
⅛ teaspoon ground cinnamon

Filling:

2 eggs
¾ cup sugar
½ teaspoon vanilla
3 tablespoons cocoa
8 ounces cream cheese
2 cups sour cream

1. Melt butter in a pie plate. Stir in remaining crust ingredients; mix well. Press crumbs to form shell. Cook on High for 1 minute. Cool completely.

2. In a blender or food processor, combine eggs, sugar, cocoa, vanilla, and cream cheese. Blend until smooth; stir in sour cream. Pour into a bowl and cook at 70% power for 4 minutes, stirring every minute.

3. Pour filling into crust. Cook at 30% power for 12 to 14 minutes. The cheesecake is done when the edge is set and slightly dull in color and the center is glossy.

4. Chill thoroughly before serving.

Black Forest Cheesecake

YIELD: ONE 8- OR 9-INCH PIE

4 (3-ounce)packages cream cheese, softened
2 eggs
½ cup sugar
1 teaspoon vanilla extract
1 Chocolate Crumb Pie Crust (see page 191)
½ cup chocolate chips, melted
1 (22-ounce) can cherry pie filling

1. In a blender or food processor, combine cream cheese, eggs, sugar, and vanilla extract. Pour into pie crust.
2. Allow chocolate to cool slightly; swirl into cream cheese mixture.
3. Bake at 70% power for 4 to 6 minutes.
4. Refrigerate until completely cooled. Top with cherry pie filling before serving.

Banana Split Pie

SERVES 6 TO 8

Crust:

2 cups crushed graham crackers
¼ cup butter or margarine, melted

Second Layer:

1 cup butter or margarine, softened
2 cups confectioners' sugar
2 eggs, room temperature

Third Layer:

3 sliced bananas

Fourth Layer:

1 (20-ounce) can crushed pineapple, well drained
1 (9-ounce) container frozen whipped topping
1 cup chopped pecans
½ cup chopped maraschino cherries

1. Mix crust ingredients well. Press into bottom of pie plate to form crust.
2. Combine ingredients for second layer and beat until stiff. Spread evenly over crust.
3. Spread sliced bananas over top of second layer.
4. Spread pineapple over bananas.
5. Cover with whipped topping.
6. Sprinkle top with nuts and cherries.
7. Refrigerate until ready to serve.

Orange Fluff Pie

SERVES 8

4 egg yolks
1 cup orange juice
1 envelope unflavored gelatin
½ cup sugar
¼ teaspoon salt
  red food coloring
2 teaspoons grated orange peel
4 egg whites
¼ cup sugar
1 Chocolate Crumb Pie Crust (see **page 191**)
  chocolate curls or sprinkles

1. Beat egg yolks in a medium-size bowl. Stir in orange juice, gelatin, ½ cup sugar, salt, and a drop of red food coloring. Cook at 70% power for 4 to 4½ minutes. Stir frequently. Mixture should be slightly thickened. Stir in orange peel.
2. Allow mixture to cool.
3. In small mixer bowl, beat egg whites until frothy. Gradually add ¼ cup sugar; beat until stiff peaks form. Carefully fold into orange mixture.
4. Pour into crust and garnish with chocolate curls. Refrigerate for at least 4 hours.

Cranberry Chiffon Pie

YIELD: ONE 9-INCH PIE

1 envelope unflavored gelatin
½ cup cold water
2 cups fresh cranberries
2 egg whites
1 cup sugar
1 tablespoon lemon juice
¼ teaspoon salt
½ cup whipping cream
1 tablespoon sugar
1 baked pie shell

1. In a large glass bowl, soften gelatin in cold water, about 5 minutes.
2. Add cranberries. Cook, covered, on High for 5 minutes, stirring once. Stir well to dissolve gelatin and set aside until cool.
3. In large electric mixer bowl, combine egg whites, 1 cup sugar, lemon juice, salt, and cranberry mixture. Beat until mixture holds stiff peaks, about 8 minutes.
4. Spoon into pie shell.
5. Chill for at least 4 hours.
6. Whip the cream with 1 tablespoon sugar and garnish top of pie.

Pumpkin Pie

YIELD: TWO 8-INCH PIES

2 cups canned pumpkin
½ teaspoon salt
1 teaspoon ground cinnamon
½ teaspoon ground ginger
¼ teaspoon ground nutmeg
¼ teaspoon ground cloves
3 eggs, beaten
¾ cup honey
1 (5.3-ounce) can evaporated milk
2 Ginger Crumb Pie Crusts (see page 192)

1. Combine pumpkin, salt and spices; add eggs, honey, and evaporated milk; mix well.
2. Pour into baked crusts.
3. Bake one pie at a time at 50% power for 18 to 20 minutes. The center will still be moist but will set up after 10 to 15 minutes' standing time.
4. Allow to cool completely before serving.

Chocolate Pie

YIELD: ONE 8- OR 9-INCH PIE

20 marshmallows
¾ cup milk
2 tablespoons cocoa
  pinch of salt
1 teaspoon vanilla
4 teaspoons rum or rum flavoring
1 cup whipping cream
1 baked pie shell
  chocale curls

1. Combine marshmallows, milk, cocoa, and salt in a large bowl. Cook on High for 3 to 4 minutes, stirring once. Stir until marshmallows are melted.
2. Stir in vanilla and rum. Cool slightly.
3. Whip cream. Fold into marshmallow mixture.
4. Pour into cooled pie shell. Refrigerate until firm. Garnish with chocolate curls.

Chocolate Crumb Pie Crust

YIELD: 1 PIE CRUST

1¼ to 1½ cups (about 20) chocolate wafer crumbs
2 tablespoons sugar
¼ cup butter

1. Place cookies in a plastic bag and crush with a rolling pin. Add sugar to the bag and mix well by working the bag with your hands.

2. Melt butter in a glass pie plate.

3. Add crushed cookies to butter; mix well. Press into the dish to form a shell. Cook on High for 1 minute.

4. Cool completely before filling.

Ginger Crumb Pie Crust

YIELD: 1 PIE CRUST

1¼ cups crushed gingersnaps
2 tablespoons sugar
¼ cup butter or margarine

1. Place cookies in a plastic bag and crush with a rolling pin. Add sugar to the bag and mix well by working the bag with your hands.

2. Melt butter in a glass pie plate.

3. Stir in sugar and gingersnaps. Mix very well to avoid lumps of sugar that will overcook. Press into dish to form shell.

4. Cook at 70% power for 1½ minutes.

5. Cool completely before filling.

Meringue Pie Shell

YIELD: 1 PIE SHELL

A meringue shell needs dry heat to cook properly, so no microwave instructions are given. However, it is very elegant when used with a filling prepared in a microwave oven.

4 egg whites
1 cup sugar
¼ teaspoon cream of tartar

Tips:

Separate eggs while cold. Beat at room temperature.
Have bowl and mixer beaters spotlessly clean and grease free.
Add sugar gradually so that it will dissolve. Check to see if meringue is too grainy by rubbing a small amount between your fingers.
Do not overbeat.

1. Line a cookie sheet with brown wrapping paper. Use the bottom of a pie plate to draw a cirlce on the paper.
2. Beat egg whites until stiff.
3. Add sugar gradually.
4. Add cream of tartar.
5. Beat until stiff and shiny.
6. Using two spatulas, spread the meringue over the circle and shape the sides. Any extra meringue can be put in a pastry bag and used to make garnishes to be baked at the same time.
7. Bake at 275° for 1 hour. Turn oven off and leave door shut for 2 hours.

Use a filling of your choice. This pie shell holds up very well in the refrigerator and need not be completely eaten the day it is made.

Cream Puffs

Puffs:

1 cup water
½ cup butter or margarine
⅛ teaspoon salt
1 cup all-purpose flour
4 eggs

Filing:

1 (3¾-ounce) package vanilla pudding
2 cups milk
1 teaspoon almond extract

Glaze:

2 ounces unsweetened chocolate
1 tablespoon butter or margarine
1 cup confectioners' sugar
2 tablespoons water

1. Puffs are made in the conventional oven. Preheat oven to 400°. Bring water, butter, and salt to a boil over high heat, stirring occasionally. Lower heat; add flour all at once. Stir rapidly until mixture forms a ball and follows spoon around pan. Remove from heat and cool slightly. Add eggs one at a time and beat until smooth. Drop from spoon onto ungreased cookie sheet. Bake 45 to 50 minutes. Cool away from drafts. When cool, cut top off and set aside. Pull out soft dough in center. (These shells can be made ahead and frozen.)

2. Combine filling ingredients in a bowl and cook on High for 6 to 7 minutes, stirring once. Cool; fill puffs.

3. Melt chocolate and butter. Add sugar and stir well. Add water and blend. Spoon over puffs at once.

Chocolate Ice Cream

YIELD: 2 QUARTS

2 cups milk
¾ cup sugar
⅛ teaspoon salt
2 eggs, beaten
2 ounces unsweetened chocolate
1 tablespoon vanilla
2 cups cream

1. Combine milk, sugar, and salt in a large bowl. Cook on High for 3 minutes.
2. With an electric mixer, beat in eggs. Be careful not to scramble them in the hot milk.
3. Cook at 50% power for 5 minutes; beat well. Continue to cook at 50% power for another 5 minutes or until mixture comes to a boil and begins to thicken; beat well. Melt chocolate and stir in.
4. Cool completely. Stir in vanilla and cream.
5. Pour into ice cream freezer and process according to manufacturer's instructions.

Choco-Peanut-Butter Ice Cream

YIELD: 2 QUARTS

1 quart half-and-half
1 cup chunky peanut butter
1 cup sugar
2 teaspoons vanilla extract
1 cup mini-chocolate bits

1. Pour the half-and-half into a 3-quart bowl. Stir in the peanut butter. Cook for about 8 minutes on High, stirring once, to scald the milk. It should begin to bubble around the edge, but do not let it boil.
2. Stir the sugar into the milk. Cool slightly.
3. Stir in the vanilla and chill mixture in the refrigerator.
4. Pour into an ice cream freezer and process according to manufacturer's instructions.

5. Put ice cream back into a large bowl and stir in the chocolate chips. Pack in an airtight container for freezing.

Bananas Foster Ice Cream

YIELD: 1½ QUARTS

1   quart half-and-half
¾   cup sugar
4   ripe bananas
1½ teaspoons ground cinnamon
1   tablespoon lemon juice
¼   cup rum

1. Pour the half-and-half into a 3-quart bowl and scald. This will take about 8 minutes on High, stirring once. It should begin to bubble around the edge, but do not let it boil.
2. Stir sugar into the milk. Cool slightly.
3. Peel the bananas and cut into chunks. In a blender or food processor, combine the bananas with 1 cup of the milk. Process until smooth.
4. To the milk in the 3-quart bowl, add the bananas, cinnamon, lemon juice, and rum. Stir well. Chill.
5. Pour into an ice cream freezer and process according to manufacturer's instructions.

Watermelon Sherbet

SERVES 8

¼   to ½ watermelon
4   cups water
2   cups sugar
1½ teaspoons to 1 tablespoon lemon juice

1. Using a very fine sieve, work with watermelon until you have extracted 2 cups of liquid.
2. Combine water and sugar and bring to a boil on High, about 8 minutes. Boil for 5 minutes.
3. Stir in watermelon juice and lemon juice to taste.

4. Pour into ice cream freezer and process according to manufacturer's instructions for ice cream.

Easy Chocolate Fudge

1 (4-ounce) package chocolate pudding mix
½ cup sugar
½ cup brown sugar
⅓ cup milk
2 tablespoons butter or margarine

1. Combine pudding mix, both sugars, and milk in a bowl. Cook on High for 5 minutes, stirring every 2 minutes.
2. Add butter without stirring and let cool for 10 minutes.
3. Stir vigorously, several minutes, until fudge begins to thicken.
4. Spread in greased dish and refrigerate until set.

Oh Boys!

YIELD: ABOUT 3 DOZEN

1 cup peanut butter
½ cup confectioners' sugar
¼ cup shredded coconut
½ cup light corn syrup
1½ cups o-shaped cereal
1 (6-ounce) package chocolate chips
⅛ teaspoon instant coffee powder

1. With an electric mixer, combine peanut butter, confectioners sugar, coconut, and syrup.
2. Stir in ceral.
3. Shape into 1-inch balls and flatten slightly.
4. In a small bowl, melt half the chocolate chips on 50% power. Stir in instant coffee powder.
5. Dip each ball in chocolate and place on cookie sheet with chocolate on top. Melt remaining chocolate as needed.
6. Refrigerate until firm. Store in refrigerator.

Rocky Road Squares

1 (12-ounce) package chocolate bits
2 tablespoons butter or margarine
1 (14-ounce) can sweetened condensed milk
2 cups dry-roasted peanuts
1 (10½-ounce) package miniature marshmallows

1. Melt chocolate at 50% power; about 3 to 5 minutes.
2. Melt butter.
3. Stir chocolate, butter, and milk together. Cool slightly.
4. Stir in marshmallows and nuts. Pour into a 13 × 9-inch dish that has been lined with waxed paper. Chill for 2 hours or until firm.
5. Remove from dish, peel off waxed paper, cut into squares. Store, covered, at room temperature.

Party Mints

3 tablespoons butter
3 tablespoons milk
1 (15.4-ounce) package creamy white frosting mix
flavoring extracts of your choice
food coloring of your choice

1. In a medium-size bowl, cook butter and milk until butter is melted.
2. Stir in frosting mix and cook on High for 1½ to 2 minutes or until bubbly.
3. Add flavoring and food coloring.
4. Spread on greased cookie sheet.
5. When set, cut into squares.
6. Store in an airtight container.

This also works well with rubber candy molds.

Sauces

Basic White Sauce

YIELD: 1 CUP

2 tablespoons butter or margarine
2 tablespoons all-purpose flour
½ teaspoon salt
    pinch of pepper, optional
1 cup milk

1. In a small bowl, combine butter, flour, salt, and pepper. Cook on High for 2 minutes, stirring once.
2. Gradually add milk, stirring. Cook on High for 3 to 4 minutes, stirring every minute, until sauce begins to thicken.
3. If it lumps, process in blender or food processor.

Instant White Sauce Mix

YIELD: 6 CUPS

1 cup flour
4 cups instant nonfat dry milk
4 teaspoons salt
1 cup butter or margarine

1. Mix flour, milk, and salt togehter.
2. Cut in butter until crumbly
3. Cover tightly and store in refrigerator.

To prepare sauce use following proportions:

Type of Sauce	Mix	Milk or	Water
thin	⅓ cup	1 cup	⅔ cup
medium	½ cup	1 cup	⅔ cup
thick	1 cup	1 cup	⅔ cup

Add grated cheese for a cheese sauce.

Easy Hollandaise Sauce

YIELD: ¾ CUP

3 egg yolks
2 tablespoons lemon juice
¼ teaspoon salt
½ cup butter or margarine, melted

1. Put egg yolks, lemon juice, and salt into a blender.
2. With blender at low speed, gradually add hot butter.
3. Blend until sauce is thickened, about 15 seconds.

Cayenne pepper, paprika, or nutmeg can be added to the sauce—in small amounts.

Milk Gravy

YIELD: ABOUT 2 CUPS

¼ cup beef or chicken drippings
¼ cup flour
¼ teaspoon salt
⅛ teaspoon pepper
1¼ cups milk

1. Put drippings in a 4-cup measure and cook on High for 1 to 2 minutes.
2. Stir in flour, salt, and pepper.
3. Gradually add milk. Cook on High for 6 to 8 minutes, stirring every minute.

Zippy Barbecue Sauce

YIELD: ABOUT 1 CUP

½ cup dark corn syrup
¼ cup catsup
⅓ cup orange juice
1   tablespoon Worcestershire sauce
1½ teaspoons steak sauce
½ teaspoon prepared mustard
1   tablespoon dried minced onion
¼ teaspoon salt
⅛ teaspoon pepper
1   tablespoon salad oil
3   to 4 drops hot sauce

1. Combine all ingredients in a 4-cup measure and mix well.

2. Cover and cook on High for 2½ minutes or until it comes to a boil. Stir; cook at 50% power for 5 minutes, stirring after 3 minutes.

Cumberland Meat Sauce

YIELD: 1⅓ CUPS

½ cup red currant jelly
½ cup orange juice
2   tablespoons lemon juice
⅛ teaspoon ground ginger
    pinch of cayenne pepper
1   tablespoon cornstarch
1½ tablespoons water

1. In a 4-cup measure combine the jelly, orange juice, lemon juice, ginger, and cayenne pepper. Cook on High for 2 minutes, stirring with a whisk after 1 minute.

2. Add cornstarch to water and stir until all lumps are gone.

3. Stir cornstarch into jelly mixture.

4. Cook on High for 1 to 1½ minutes or until the mixture begins to boil. Boil on High for 1 minute. Sauce should be nicely thickened.

5. Serve warm over slices of beef, poultry, or ham.

Taco Sauce

2 (15-ounce) cans tomato sauce
4 long yellow banana peppers (sold in jars)
1 medium onion
½ green pepper
1 teaspoon oregano
1 tablespoon chili powder

1. Combine all ingredients in a blender or food processor. Process until ingredients are chopped fine.
2. Extra juice that the banana peppers were packed in can be added for additional hotness.
3. Store in the refrigerator.

Maple Syrup

YIELD: ABOUT 2 CUPS

1 cup hot water
2 cups sugar
1 teaspoon maple flavoring

1. Bring water to a boil.
2. Stir in sugar until dissolved.
3. Add maple flavoring. Cook 1 to 2 minutes on High, stirring once.
4. Store in the refrigerator.

Hard Sauce

1 cup unsalted butter, softened

1 cup confectioners' sugar
   brandy flavoring

1. Cream butter and sugar together.
2. Add brandy flavoring to taste.
3. Beat until fluffy.
4. Store in refrigerator.

Lemon Sauce

YIELD: ABOUT 1½ CUPS

½ cup sugar
1½ tablespoons cornstarch
1 cup lukewarm water
   peel of 1 lemon, grated
2 tablespoons lemon juice

1. In a 4-cup measure combine sugar and cornstarch.
2. Gradually stir in water.
3. Cook on High for 3 to 4 minutes, stirring every minute. Sauce should thicken and become translucent.
4. Stir in lemon peel and lemon juice.
5. Store in refrigerator and reheat when needed.

Butterscotch Sauce

YIELD: ABOUT ¾ CUP

⅓ cup light corn syrup
¾ cup brown sugar, packed firm
2 tablespoons butter
⅛ teaspoon salt
⅓ cup evaporated milk

1. Combine corn syrup, brown sugar, butter, and salt in a bowl. Cook on High until syrup teaches a soft ball stage, about 2½ minutes.
2. Cool completely.
3. Stir in evaporated milk.
4. Serve hot or cold.

Hot Fudge Sauce

YIELD: ABOUT 1 CUP

2 ounces unsweetened chocolate
1 tablespoon butter
⅓ cup hot water
1 cup sugar
2 tablespoons light corn syrup

1. Melt chocolate at 50% power, about 3 minutes.
2. Melt butter.
3. Stir all ingredients together. Cook at 50% power for 3 minutes or until sauce boils. Continue to cook at 50% power for 3 to 4 minutes, stirring at least once or twice.
4. Pour over ice cream.

Index